PORTRAITS OF

Nathaniel Hawthorne.

PORTRAITS OF

Nathaniel Hawthorne.

RITA K. •AN ICONOGRAPHY• GOLLIN

NORTHERN ILLINOIS UNIVERSITY PRESS

For Dick, Kathy, Michael, Jim, and Steve

This book could not have been completed without the help of two generous men: C. E. Frazer Clark, Jr., who shared the treasures of his Hawthorne collection, and Neal Smith, who provided typescripts of Hawthorne's correspondence prepared for the Centenary edition. I am also grateful to other friends and colleagues who read the book in manuscript and helped me approach the goals of accuracy and completeness—among them Dan Fink, Walter Harding, Buford Jones, James Mellow, Robert Sobieszek, and Thomas Woodson. My searches were facilitated by librarians of the Berg Collection of the New York Public Library, the Boston Public Library, the Concord Free Public Library, the Essex Institute, the Frick Art Reference Library, the Library of Congress, and the Massachusetts Historical Society. The Geneseo Foundation helped defray the expense of preparing photographs. And, as always, I relied on the sound counsel and generous criticism of my husband, Richard Gollin.

Library of Congress Cataloging in Publication Data
Gollin, Rita K., 1928–
   Portraits of Nathaniel Hawthorne.
   Bibliography: p.
   1. Hawthorne, Nathaniel, 1804–1864—Portraits, etc.
2. Biography—19th century—Portraits. 3. Portraits.
I. Title.
PS1885.G64   1983   813'.3   83-12155
ISBN 0–87580–087–4

Copyright © 1983 by Northern Illinois University Press
Published by Northern Illinois University Press,
DeKalb, Illinois 60115
Manufactured in the United States of America

This book was set in Garamond
The Editor was Leslie Wildrick
The Designer was Joan Westerdale
The Book was printed and bound by Thomson-Shore, Dexter, Michigan

Contents

Illustrations

Illustrations

Chronology of Portraits

This chart lists all known life portraits of Hawthorne, most of the portrayals derived from them during his lifetime, and the most important of the posthumous portrayals. An asterisk (*) signifies publication in this volume. Boldface type signifies an original image; derived images are given immediately afterward.

Portraits	Date	Artist	Location or Publication	Special Comments
Silhouette*	1825(?)	Unknown	One copy at Bowdoin College and another in collection of Manning Hawthorne	Perhaps made on the occasion of Hawthorne's graduation from Bowdoin College.
Miniature*	1836(?)	Unknown	Unknown	Known only through photocopy in collection of C. E. Frazer Clark, Jr. (Portrait suspect because of moustache.)
Pencil Sketch*	1838(?)	Sophia Hawthorne	In Hawthorne family album, owned by Manning Hawthorne (p. 8)	Perhaps the drawing by Sophia Peabody in her family's Salem parlor in December 1838, though a pencilled note in Rose's hand assigns it to the Hawthornes' "early married life."
Oil Painting*	1840	Charles Osgood	Essex Institute, Salem	First oil painting of Hawthorne, made by Salem's foremost portraitist. Perhaps commissioned by Hawthorne's uncle Robert Manning.
Etching*	1884	Stephen Alonzo Schoff	*Nathaniel Hawthorne and His Wife,* 2 vols. (Boston: James R. Osgood, 1884), II: frontispiece	Prepared for publication in Julian Hawthorne's biography but also issued as a separate print.
Daguerreotype Miniature	1841	A. S. Southworth	Unknown	First known daguerreotype of Hawthorne, mentioned by Sophia in letter to him.
Crayon Drawing*	1846	Eastman Johnson	Craigie House, Cambridge	One of a series commissioned by Henry Wadsworth Longfellow.
Portrait Sketch(?)	1847	Charles Martin	Unknown	Hawthorne agreed to sit for sketch intended as basis for newspaper woodcut, but neither sketch nor woodcut have been located.

Chronology of Portraits

Daguerreotype*	1848(?)	John A. Whipple	Library of Congress	Either the original half-plate or a copy by Mathew Brady, made before 1855 and perhaps in 1848.
Wood Engraving*	1855	J. Barry	*Ballou's Pictorial Drawing-Room Companion*, 9 (1855): 36	First publication of a Hawthorne engraving based on a daguerreotype, identified as "by Whipple and Black."
Wood Engraving*	1858	Unknown	*Illustrated London News*, 32 (1858): 256	Small print (3 inches high), included with brief account of Hawthorne's career.
Wood Engraving*	1886	Thomas Johnson	*Century*, 10 (1886): frontispiece	Date of original daguerreotype given as 1848.
Oil Painting*	1850	Cephas Thompson	Grolier Club, New York	Made at artist's request. Purchased by Ticknor as gift to Hawthorne. Discussed in *American Notebooks*.
Steel Engraving*	1851	Thomas Phillibrown	*Twice-told Tales* (Boston: Ticknor, Reed, and Fields, 1851), frontispiece	Commissioned by Ticknor and Co. First engraving of Hawthorne and first to appear in a book. Used by other engravers.
Wood Engraving*	1851	Albert (or Alfred) Bobbett and Charles Edmonds, from drawing by Samuel Wallin	*International Magazine of Literature, Art, and Science*, 3 (1851): 156	First engraving in a monthly magazine.
Same as above			*National Magazine*, 2 (1853): 17	No acknowledgement that this is a second appearance.
Wood Engraving*	1851	John William Orr	*Boston Museum*, 4 (1851): 1	One of first known wood engravings and the first to appear in a weekly magazine.
Wood Engraving	1852	C. Simms	*Twice-told Tales* (London: George Routledge, 1852), frontispiece	Hawthorne said the portrait in this pirated edition was "awful."
Wood Engraving*	1853	Unknown	*Little Annie's Ramble* (Halifax: Milner and Sowerby, 1853), frontispiece	In pirated edition which Hawthorne saw and bought for the "queer" portrait.
Wood Engraving	1855	W. Roberts	*Cyclopedia of American Literature* (New York: Scribner, 1855), II: 506	Hawthorne agreed to be "carbonadoed by Duyckinck" in 1851.
Postage Stamp	1983	Designed by Bradbury Thompson	Issued 8 July in Salem	Twenty-cent stamp in Literary Arts Series.
Miniature	1852	Mrs. Daniel Steele	Unknown	In April, Hawthorne agreed to sit for miniature, commissioned by famous actress Charlotte Cushman.

Chronology of Portraits

Three Daguerreo-types	1852	Unknown	Unknown	In July, Sophia told her father that a daguerreotypist "seized" Hawthorne and made three "somewhat good" pictures.
Oil Painting*	1852	George P. A. Healy	New Hampshire Historical Society	Commissioned by Franklin Pierce for $1,000 before his inauguration as President. The only oil portrait not etched or engraved for publication.
Group Photograph*	1856	Philip Delamotte	One copy in Bancroft Library, University of California at Berkeley, and another in the Bodleian Library at Oxford	First photograph made in England, first as participant in group photograph, first outdoor photograph, and the first one whose negative Hawthorne saw. Discussed in *English Notebooks*.
Group Photograph*	1857	"Mr. Keith" or "Mr. Berry"	Liverpool Record Office	Only known photograph of Hawthorne as American Consul participating in a public ceremony. Mentioned in *English Notebooks*.
Photograph(?)	1857(?)	Unknown	Unknown	Hawthorne agreed to sit at Fry's request, but no further information is available.
Crayon Drawing	1858	Fanny Hawarth	Unknown	Hawthorne noted in diary on 21 July 1858 that she "came & sketched a crayon-portrait of me—for herself."
Marble Bust	1858(?)	"Phillips"	Unknown	Reported by Moncure Conway, *Life of Nathaniel Hawthorne*, p. 199.
Marble Bust*	1858	Louisa Lander	Concord Free Public Library	Hawthorne agreed to sit at Lander's request and paid for the bust but disliked it (although he had enjoyed the sittings, discussed in his notebooks, and said the clay model had "highest praise"). Hawthorne's first sculptured portrait, and the only one he purchased.
Sketches*	1859	Julian Hawthorne	Sketchbook in the Bancroft Library, Berkeley	Three small pencil sketches and two in watercolor made by thirteen-year-old Julian in sketchbook shared with his mother. The first images of Hawthorne with a moustache.
Three Photographs (see below)	1860	J. J. E. Mayall	Various Collections	Taken before the Hawthornes left England, though Hawthorne reportedly denied their existence, and friends disagreed about their number and the occasion.

Chronology of Portraits

"Bright-Motley" pose*				According to Henry Bright, chosen by him from a group of photographs made at his request. Copy requested by Sophia after Hawthorne's death as one of her favorites.
Wood Engraving*	1865	Unknown	*Good Company for Every Day in the Year* (Boston: Ticknor and Fields, 1866), opposite p. 288	Engraving of Sophia's copy commissioned by Fields that she thought "soulless." First American publication of a Mayall image.
Wood Engraving	1871	Unknown	James D. McCabe, Jr., *Great Fortunes and How They Were Made ...* (Philadelphia: George McLean, 1871), Section 9, chapter 34, p. 579	Image reversed; reprinted in *Great Fortunes* and in *Kings of Fortune*, ed. W. R. Houghton—six reprintings in the course of twenty years.
Wood Engraving*	1872	Unknown	*Harper's New Monthly Magazine*, 45 (1872): 683	Reprinted in 1886; also issued as a separate print. First publication of a Mayall image in a periodical.
Lithograph	1883	Joseph E. Baker	Various Collections	Published by Houghton Mifflin in life-sized print designed for use in schools, and also in smaller sizes. First lithograph of a Hawthorne image, and one of the best known portraits.
Etching*	1884	Stephen Alonzo Schoff	*Nathaniel Hawthorne and His Wife*, II: 150	Prepared for publication in Julian Hawthorne's biography but also issued as a separate print.
Etching	1886	W. B. P. Closson	*Homes and Haunts of the Poets* (Boston: Prang, 1886)	Published as a separate sheet in portfolio.
Etching*	Unknown	Thomas Johnson	Example in National Gallery	Signed in plate and on print "T. Johnson." Issued by J. O. Wright.
Line Engraving*	Unknown	Unknown	Example in National Gallery	Engraved by H. B. Hall and Sons and printed by James H. Lamb.
Wood Engraving	1956	Ben Shahn	Vintage Jubilee edition of Hawthorne's short stories (New York: Viking, 1956), frontispiece	
"Holden" pose*				According to Mayall's records, copy sent to John Lothrop Motley in May 1860. Mayall, Jr., discovered original print and negative in 1886 and issued copies.
Wood Engraving	1864	Unknown	English edition of *Our Old Home* (1864)	Identified only through Hall Scrapbook; criticized by Hall and Mayall, Jr., but possibly first publication of a Mayall image.

Chronology of Portraits

White-line Wood Engraving*	1886	Thomas Johnson	*Harper's*, 73 (1886): 164	Frontispiece to July issue.
Photogravure	1886	Unknown	Published in "commercial catalogues"	According to Mayall, Jr., the plate he commissioned was stolen by an engraver, who published it.
Bronze Medallion	1892	Ringel D'Illzach	Model and example in Grolier Club	Illustrated in leaflet of 14 February 1893, offering the bas relief for sale at ten dollars.
Wood Engraving*	1894	"T. V."	*Harper's*, 89 (1894): 164	Included in Howells's account of first meeting of Hawthorne and other New England writers.
"Bennoch" pose*				According to Bennoch, selected in Hawthorne's presence in May 1860, and his "best likeness."
Line Engraving*	1873	Oliver Pelton	*Eclectic*, 81 (1873): 129	
Line Engraving*	1879	Unknown	Example in Library of Congress	Published by New York firm of E. Dexter.
Crayon Drawing	1880 or 1881	Fred Piercy	Unknown	According to Bennoch, life-sized drawing copied from photograph.
Retouched Photographs	1881	Fred Piercy	Unknown	According to Bennoch, Piercy prepared copies for sale.
Oil Painting*	1886	Alexander Johnston	Bowdoin College	Commissioned by Bennoch and given to the college.
White-line Wood Engraving*	1887	Timothy Cole	*Century*, 11 (1887): 818	Frontispiece to April issue and issued as Plate XXIII in *Century Gallery of One Hundred Portraits*.
Oil Painting	1898(?)	A. E. Smith		
Photoengraving	1898	Unknown	*Das Neunzehnte Jahrhundert in Bildnissen* (1899), p. 3	Copyright by Foster Brothers and issued in various sizes.
Marble Medallion*	1860	Edward J. Kuntze	Plaster cast at New-York Historical Society	Purchased by Hawthorne admirers in England and sent to him in 1862; disliked and perhaps destroyed by Sophia.
Pencil Sketch*	1861	Una Hawthorne	Berg Collection of New York Public Library	Sketch of left profile, mounted in oval cardboard frame.
Pencil Sketch*	1861	Julian Hawthorne	Berg Collection of New York Public Library	Sketch of left profile, on a sheet of paper with another sketch on the back.

Chronology of Portraits

Pencil Sketch*	1861(?)	Sophia Hawthorne?	Hawthorne Family album, owned by Manning Hawthorne	Sketch of partial right profile, more accomplished than other sketches by family members.
Photograph of Hawthorne and Sophia*	1861(?)	Unknown	*Nathaniel Hawthorne and His Circle* (New York: Harper, 1903), p. 58	Probably taken in the spring of 1861, across the road from the Wayside.
Three Photographs (see below)	1861	Silsbee and Case	Various Collections	Hawthorne sat at the photographers' request, perhaps in mid-December for all three.
Seated Pose*		W. H. Getchell	Various Collections	One of Sophia's favorite photographs; detailed account of tedious sitting.
Crayon Drawing	1865	Samuel W. Rowse	Unknown	Commissioned by Fields.
Copy of Crayon Drawing*	Unknown	Unknown	Craigie House, Cambridge	Longfellow's copy.
Line Engraving*	1883	J. A. J. Wilcox	Frontispiece to twelfth volume of Riverside Edition, in *Hawthorne Portfolio*, and in various collections	Artist famous for portraits.
Line Engraving*	Unknown	Hezekiah Wright Smith	Example at Baltimore Museum of Art	Artist famous for portraits.
Line Engraving*	Unknown	Henri Emile Lefort	Examples at Grolier Club and Baltimore Museum of Art	Medal-winning French artist.
White-line Wood Engraving*	1886	Unknown	*Century*, 10 (1886): 93	Illustrating Julian Hawthorne on "Hawthorne's Philosophy."
Oil Painting	1893	H. Frances Osborne	Essex Institute	Artist's gift.
Statue*	1925	Bela Lyon Pratt	Hawthorne Boulevard, Salem	Commissioned by Hawthorne Memorial Association, cast by Gorham Company.
Seated Pose*		W. H. Getchell	Examples owned by C. E. Frazer Clark, Jr.	Apparently taken at the same sitting as pose listed above, perhaps the one Sophia considered "bad." Relatively unknown.
Seated Pose*		Unknown	Example given by Hawthornes to former nursemaid Dora Golden, now owned by Barbara Bacheler	Hawthorne holds the same hat as in the first of these poses (listed above) but wears a different coat than in either one; perhaps taken in Silsbee and Case studio at a different time, though possibly in another studio. Relatively unknown.

Chronology of Portraits

Five Photographs (see below)	1861 or 1862	James Wallace Black	Various Collections	Possibly taken on the same occasion, before Hawthorne's trip to Washington.
Seated Poses*				Nearly identical; one relatively unknown.
Standing Pose*				
Bronze Bust*	1939	Daniel Chester French	Hall of Fame	Sculptor might have used additional Boston photographs.
Standing Poses, Hawthorne with Ticknor and Fields*				Two photographs almost identical: the only group studio photographs, the only ones of Hawthorne with his publishers, the only ones of Hawthorne wearing a hat (all three men are wearing top hats).
"Field-Marshal" Photograph*	1861(?)	John A. Whipple?	Unknown	Sophia praised Whipple's speed at time of Getchell sitting.
Imperial "Head"	1864	John A. Whipple	Unknown	Sophia had mixed response to large-scale portrait, commissioned by Fields.
Etching*	1884	Stephen Alonzo Schoff	*Nathaniel Hawthorne and His Wife*, II: 300	Julian identified the original photograph as one Fields called the "Field-Marshal."
Engraving*	1897	John Andrew & Son	Rose Hawthorne Lathrop, *Memories of Hawthorne* (Boston: Houghton, Mifflin, 1897): frontispiece	
Engraving	1899	John Andrew & Son	Annie Fields, *Nathaniel Hawthorne* (Boston: Small and Maynard, 1899), frontispiece	Photogravure identified as from an 1862 photograph by Black; almost no hair on crown, and almost identical to above.
Stereograph	1862	Unknown	Unknown	Hawthorne said he was "seized" for a "stereoscope" in New York en route to Washington and saw the fearfully "like" negative.
Four Photographs (see below)	1862	Alexander Gardner for Mathew Brady	Various Collections	Sittings for Ticknor and Hawthorne arranged by friend during Washington visit; Hawthorne promised a free Imperial.
Seated Pose, jacket unbuttoned*			National Portrait Gallery	

Wood Engraving	1870	John Karst, drawing by H. L. Spread	*Appleton's Journal of Literature, Science, and Art,* 9 (1870): 405	Image is reversed and jaw distorted; reprinted in the *Critic* in 1881, 1894, 1897, and 1898 and in the *Bookman* in 1897.
Seated Pose, jacket buttoned*			Library of Congress, National Archives, National Portrait Gallery	
Wood Engraving	1887	Unknown	*Portraits and Biographical Sketches of Twenty American Authors* (Boston: Houghton Mifflin, 1887), preceding the two-page Hawthorne sketch	An "extra number" of the Riverside Literature Series, intended for use in the schools.
Wood Engraving	1899	Unknown	Donald Mitchell, *American Lands and Letters* (New York: Scribner's, 1899) p. 261	Identified as "From a photograph given by Hawthorne to the author in the Spring of 1862."
Half-tone Photoengraving	1904	Harry Davidson	*Century,* 46 (1904): 350	
Standing "Napoleonic" Pose*			National Portrait Gallery; Minute Man National Historic Park, Concord; Bowdoin College	
Wood Engraving	1887	G. Reynolds	*Bookman,* 6 (1897): 331	Poor likeness dated 1887 and identified as "From a wash drawing by G. Reynolds after a daguerreotype believed to have been taken in the last year of his life. Now reproduced for the first time."
Wood Engraving	1899	Unknown	*American Lands and Letters,* p. 259	Faithful likeness showing entire pose.
Standing Pose*			Library of Congress	Vignetted glass negative.
Oil Painting*	1862	Emanuel Leutze	National Portrait Gallery	Painted at artist's request in Washington.
White-line Wood Engraving*	1894	Richard George Tietze	*Century,* 27 (1894): 97	Signed in the block.
Granite Bust	1896	Jonathan S. Hartley	Library of Congress portico	Described and pictured in *Harper's Weekly* 9(1896): 1043.
Composite India Ink Drawing, "Washington Irving and His Literary Friends at Sunnyside"	1860	F. O. C. Darley	Unknown	Commissioned by Derby Galleries, New York.
Oil Painting	1863	Christian Schussele	Sunnyside, Washington Irving's home in Tarrytown, New York	Exhibited at Derby Galleries.

Chronology of Portraits

Oil Painting*	1864	Christian Schussele	National Portrait Gallery	
Line and Stipple Engraving	1863	Thomas Oldham Barlow	Essex Institute, Massachusetts Historical Society, and others	Sold to subscribers by Irving Publishing Company.
Ivory Miniature*	1862 or after	Peter Kramer	Butler Library, Columbia University	Delicately painted on ivory.

Notes

On Portrait Sizes

In accordance with established convention, dimensions of photographs are given width first, but all other portraits are given height first.

On Documentation

Citations to Hawthorne's works are from the Centenary Edition (Columbus, Ohio: Ohio State University Press, 1962–) and are given parenthetically, as follows: *The House of the Seven Gables* (1965) (*HSG*); *The Marble Faun* (1968) (*MF*); *The American Notebooks* (1972) (*AN*); *Twice-told Tales* (1974) (*T-tT*); *Mosses from an Old Manse* (1974) (*Mosses*); *The French and Italian Notebooks* (1980) (*FIN*), except for the *English Notebooks* (*EN*), which is from the Modern Language Association 1941 edition, edited by Randall Stewart. Letters are quoted from typescripts prepared for the forthcoming Centenary Edition and given by date.

Unless otherwise indicated, information about artists is from George C. Groce and David A. Wallace, *The New-York Historical Society's Dictionary of Artists in America, 1564–1860* (New Haven: Yale University Press, 1957); or James F. Carr, *Mantle Fielding's Dictionary of American Painters, Sculptors, and Engravers* (New York: James F. Carr, 1965).

On Correspondence

Letters to George H. Holden from Francis Bennoch are in the library of the University of Virginia; letters to Holden from Julian Hawthorne and from the editors of *Harper's* and *Century* are in the collection of C. E. Frazer Clark, Jr.; letters to Henry A. Bright from Sophia Hawthorne and James T. Fields are quoted by Robert C. Hall in his Scrapbook, now in the Berg Collection of the New York Public Library, which also includes his letters from J. J. E. Mayall, Jr., and Francis Bennoch; letters to Charles Henry Hart about Hawthorne's portraits from Julian Hawthorne, Rose Hawthorne Lathrop, and others are included in the Charles Henry Hart Papers, Archives of American Art, Smithsonian Institution, Anon. Gift, 1971, Roll 930. The letters of Sophia Hawthorne to Annie Fields and James T. Fields are transcribed from manuscripts in the Boston Public Library, unless otherwise indicated.

Introduction

"In fact, there is no such thing as a true portrait; they are all delusions; and I never saw any two alike, nor, hardly, any two that I could recognize, merely by the portraits themselves, as being of the same man. A bust has more reality."

(*The American Notebooks*, p. 491)

Frequently in the fiction of Nathaniel Hawthorne, someone is looking intently at a face, trying to understand what lies behind it. Sometimes he is staring at his own reflection, as does the sentimental boy in "The Vision of the Fountain," the wry narrator of "Monsieur du Miroir," and the agonized Dimmesdale: each ponders questions about his own identity. But if the character is staring at a portrait, questions about art as well as life arise, questions about how accurately a portrait can at once fix a sitter's physical appearance and suggest his "secret character."

In his letters and notebooks, Hawthorne sometimes raised such questions about his own portraits. What is surprising is not that he asked the questions, but that he could address them to so many portraits. Hawthorne was an unusually handsome man, but also an unusually modest man. Yet he repeatedly sat for his portrait not only because the idea of such "earthly immortality" fascinated him but also because of his sense of obligation to his family, his friends, his publishers, and his readers. He regarded most of these portraits with wry amusement, observing that the face he saw in the mirror each day eluded any artist who tried to give it fixed form. Many of the "likenesses" dismayed him, though he made no serious complaints. Nobody but Sophia could presume to know his eternal visage, he believed, and even the most skillful artist could only convey intimations of his complex identity.

The Image of Hawthorne

Undoubtedly, the portraits do tell us what Hawthorne looked like. Contemporary descriptions of a handsome Hawthorne with luminous eyes and waving brown hair are amply confirmed by four oil paintings—the Osgood of 1840, the Thompson of 1850, the Healy of 1852, and the Leutze of 1862. The color of those famous eyes must have been remarkably elusive: they appear to be light gray in the Osgood, gray-green in the Thompson, dark gray in Healy's portrait, and blue-gray in Leutze's.[1] But all the portraits agree about his other features—his high forehead, deep-set eyes, thick eyebrows, straight nose, and full lips. Viewed in sequence, Hawthorne's portraits provide a vivid sense of his personal identity. We observe the beauty of his young manhood developing into maturity, then the startlingly rapid depredations of his last years. A few things remain relatively constant: the "wonderful eyes," the dignified posture, and the clothing that was virtually a uniform.

Most of Hawthorne's readers keep two pictures of him in mind at the same time: he is at once the handsome, clean-shaven man of the early paintings and the bitter old man with a moustache of the last photographs. The double image seems particularly appropriate for a writer who was always concerned about process and change. Yet there is some danger of oversimplification: some of the last images of Hawthorne show him relaxed and unperturbed, even when restricted by the photographers' mechanical contrivances, and one of his sternest images is the relatively early daguerreotype. In his portraits, as in his writings, Hawthorne evades easy generalizations.

Yet looking at pictures of him, we recognize his public image as both a symbolic construct and a practical choice. We soon become familiar with the conservative garb he usually wore in public: a long black jacket, a shawl-collared vest, and a black silk bow-tied stock worn with a high-collared white shirt. The clothing clearly suggests dignity and propriety but also frugality and relative indifference to style. Photographs of the last years show only minor variations: sometimes the coat is double-breasted, sometimes with a velvet collar; sometimes Hawthorne is dressed for the outdoors in a top hat and overcoat; and occasionally he holds a round-crowned and wide-brimmed hat (probably the "soft, brown felt hat" his daughter Rose recalled he bought in Italy) and wearing his brown "double-decked" broadcloth Talma overcoat.[2] Of course, he did not always dress somberly. At Brook Farm he wore thin pantaloons, workshirts, a blue wool "frock," and thick-soled cowhide boots. For writing, he liked to wear a dressing gown. Julian clearly remembered the purple and gold paisley robe his father wore in his Mall Street study, which had a red lining stained on the left where his father wiped his pen.[3] But neither in this gown nor in his farmer's clothes would Hawthorne put himself on public display, as he explained to Longfellow in the course of figuring out the appropriate costume to wear for a newspaper sketch:

A dressing gown would be the best, for an author;— but I cannot wear mine to Boston. I once possessed a blue woollen frock, which saw much service at Brook Farm and Concord, and in which I once went to Brighton to buy pigs. Gladly would I appear before men and angels in that garment; but on leaving the Manse, I bequeathed it to Ellery Channing. In a dress-coat, I should look like a tailor's pattern, (which certainly is not characteristic of my actual presence;)—so that I think I shall show myself in a common sack, with my stick in one hand and hat in the other.[4]

As a bachelor, Hawthorne had relied on his family to take care of his clothing. His mother and sisters made some of his clothes—shirts, pantaloons, and stocks—and took charge of others. When he was at Brook Farm in June 1841, for example, Louisa wrote him that his stocks were "in progress," his mother was

sewing buttons on three pairs of thin pantaloons, his frock-coat had been sent out to be dyed, and she wondered if he needed any more "working-shirts."[5] The making of stocks continued even after his marriage: Hawthorne asked Louisa on 20 May 1851, "Can you make me a black silk stock, to be ready when I come?"[6]

But evidently Sophia took charge of her husband's wardrobe. Writing to her mother in January 1846, she reported on her husband's splendid new dressing gown and her own efficiency: "I have almost arranged his wardrobe for a year to come, so that he can begin all over new again."[7] A request she made to her mother two months later, just after Hawthorne was appointed Surveyor of the Salem Custom House, gives precise detail about his formal public attire:

*Will you ask father to go to Earle's and order for Mr. Hawthorne a suit of clothes: the coat to be broadcloth six or seven dollars a yard; the pantaloons of kersey-mere or broadcloth of quality to correspond; and the vest of stain,—**all to be black**?*[8]

In such a suit of clothes, Hawthorne went on view at the Custom House and in artists' studios.

Even in the country Hawthorne dressed essentially the same way, but with an important difference; and a letter written from Lenox to his Salem friend Zachariah Burchmore in March 1851 makes it clear that the choice was his. Enclosing a piece of string that gave his measurements, he asked "Zach" to buy him panta-loons from "a cheap clothing establishment" made "of some stout dark cloth, suited to the gravity of my character," a comparable vest, and a pair of "de Coen's three-dollar boots: for I can find none hereabouts that will last half as long." Hawthorne was explicit about his motives: "It would be nonsense to go to the expense of John Earle's prices" for country dressing, but he wanted to go on looking "grave and respectable." For the same reasons he asked Louisa to make a silk stock two months later, even suggesting that instead of sending it in a package she should "keep it till I come, for fear of its being jammed."[9]

In important respects, Hawthorne's attitude toward clothing was as practical as Thoreau's. He wanted everything to be inexpensive, durable, and comfortable. Fashion was never at issue. But unlike Thoreau, Hawthorne worried about public opinion: he was a showman arranging his costume to make a good impression at the same time that he made fun of himself for doing so. In a curious way, Hawthorne stopped the clock: he would change, but the gravity and respectability of his costume would remain the same.

Approaching Hawthorne through his portraits, we see him more clearly than before and also understand him better. He emerges as an unusually agreeable, patient, and practical man. Whether a friend or a stranger asked him to sit for a portrait, he did not refuse; and whether for a painter, a sculptor, or a photographer, he endured long sittings. He remained docile while strapped into a "mechanical contrivance" in the Silsbee and Case studios, Sophia reported, letting the photographer pivot him and arrange his hair, though he hated being touched. He knew that in a sense he was being published, fixed by the artist.

Several of his best known portraits were made at the direct request of artists who speculated that they could sell them, and did. Cephas Thompson and Emanuel Leutze painted him, Louisa Lander modeled a bust of him, and Kuntze fixed his profile on a medallion. Sometimes he sat to gratify a friend or admirer: Eastman Johnson made his crayon portrait for Longfellow, Healy his oil painting for Pierce, Mrs. Steele a miniature for Charlotte Cushman, and Fanny Hawarth made a drawing "for herself."[10] Often the artists were his wife and children, and once he agreed to pose for a photograph that he knew Sophia would want. But usually when he sat for photographs, his motive was essentially practical; they were a condition of literary celebrity. Not only did he need small photographs for distribution to friends, but photographers required them for sale to the general public. Hawthorne therefore let himself be "seized" for a daguerreotype in Boston in 1852 and for a stereograph in New York a decade later; he granted the "urgent request" of Silsbee and Case to sit in their studio, and the three photographs of Hawthorne alone and two with his publishers made at Black's studio were probably taken at the request of the photographer or the publishers. He was a writer, so his face was in the public domain.

In still another sense, sitting for portraits expressed Hawthorne's practicality: he was fascinated with process, with the way an individual's features could emerge on canvas or in clay or in a photograph. In Thompson's studio he paid attention to the "pictorial chair," the lighting, and the artist's modes of procedure; in Lander's studio, he watched the clay take shape and the workmen translate clay into marble. Similarly, he approached photography as a technological process, though without losing sight of philosophical issues. A key conversation in *The House of the Seven Gables* concerns the issue of whether the daguerreotype or "sun picture" could ever lie. And in his *English Notebooks* Hawthorne recorded his experience in an Oxford garden where he watched a photographer arrange his plates and his subjects, then saw the reversed negative image emerge, fixed in time, and recognized his own image strangely "apart" from himself.

Hawthorne and Portraiture

Hawthorne's special interest in portraits can be explained in terms of need and opportunity. Most broadly, it was conjoined to his fundamental concern with character and identity, whether concealed or manifest, fixed or fluid, but always seen in a social context. As a writer, he defined character through physical details, primarily details of physiognomy and expression.[11] Obviously, portraits would interest him more than (for example) landscapes or genre paintings.

His reading fed that interest. From childhood on, Hawthorne encountered portraits as a stock device in Gothic fiction. In Walpole's *Castle of Otranto* and Mrs. Radcliffe's romances, for example, portraits served as agents of terror and messengers from the past. They might become mysteriously dislodged, their eyes or lips might move, or their postures might change, frightening the hero, the heroine, and the reader. Hawthorne drew on the device but greatly extended it in his own fiction.

While growing up in Salem, he took portraits as a part of ordinary experience. It is true that in Salem houses and Boston galleries, he encountered historical and sacred paintings by contemporary Americans alongside copies of European masterpieces, and gift books and magazines published engravings of works in every genre. But for Hawthorne, as for most New Englanders, the most familiar kind of painting was the portrait, especially the family portrait.

In his notebook for 1837, he recorded a visit to Salem's Essex Historical Society, where he looked at time-darkened portraits of Governor Leverett, Sir William Pepperell, John Endecott, William Pynchon, and Oliver Cromwell, as well as at a group of peeling, yellow-faced miniatures and "half a dozen, or more, family portraits of the Olivers." Characteristically, Hawthorne displayed detached curiosity about his cultural heritage, coupled with a readiness to move from detailed observation to thoughtful generalization.

What most struck him was the detail of the costume: "The dresses, embroidery, laces &c, of the Oliver family are generally done better than the faces." And this provoked a further generalization: "Nothing gives a stronger idea of old worm-eaten aristocracy, of a family's being crazy with age, and its being time that it was extinct, than these black, dusty, faded, antique-dressed portraits, such as those of the Oliver family."[12] Hawthorne was repelled by the deterioration of the portraits (as he would be repelled by darkened, faded, peeling paintings in the galleries of England and Italy), but this was not only a matter of aesthetics. He read the conjunction of material decay and attention to clothing as a symbolic statement about what went wrong with New England's aristocracy.

A tombstone in Ipswich provoked a similar, if lighter-hearted, response in 1835, though the portrait on it had withstood the wrack of time. Hawthorne described the figure: a minister, "about a third the size of life, carved in relief, with his cloak, bands, and wig, in excellent preservation; all the buttons of his waistcoat &c being done with great minuteness; the ministers nose on a level with his cheeks." Hawthorne was amused by the idea of a carver who expended his skill on buttons (and he would repeat this response in Rome twenty-three years later). His description ends with a mocking pun: "It was an upright grave stone."[13]

Such specific description by Hawthorne is rare, but whenever he wrote about works of art in his notebooks he was usually writing about portraits and what they might communicate. Over a year after the Ipswich entry, he recorded a random thought: "It would be a good idea for a painter to paint a picture of a great actor, representing him in several different characters of one scene—as Iago and Othello, for instance"—a provocative idea about capturing an individual's deliberate dissimulations that he would later apply to Judge Pyncheon. But if expression could be artful, features could not; and Hawthorne's interest in physiognomy as destiny is evident in another notebook entry, the germ for "The Great Stone Face": "The semblance of a human face to be formed on the side of a mountain, or in the fracture of a small stone, by a lusus nature ... and by and by, a boy is born, whose features gradually assume the aspect of that portrait." A complicated anecdote that Elizabeth Peabody once told him anticipates "Drowne's Wooden Image" as well as passages in *The House of the Seven Gables* and *The Marble Faun*, the tale of a judge so beautiful that many women wore his miniature portrait until they died and who had modeled for a statue of Apollo that came to life when an admirer kissed it. Perhaps Hawthorne's most characteristic notebook comment is about visitors to a wax museum, including "myself, who examine wax faces and flesh ones with equal interest." But even a casual notation about a famous carver of tombstone cherubs which bore "the likeness of the deceased" suggests his interest in the kinds of truth a "likeness" might suggest.[14] He was fascinated by any effort to impose the fixity of portraiture on the flux of mortality.

In this context we can appreciate the entry in Hawthorne's notebook written about a year after he first met Sophia Peabody: "S. A. P.—taking my likeness." When she entered his life near the end of 1837, Sophia broadened his responsiveness to portraiture as well as to other modes of art. A few years before, her portrait sketches had impressed her hosts in Cuba, and a different kind of portrait sealed her intimacy with Hawthorne, a Flaxman-style outline drawing of the hero of "The Gentle Boy." Offering it to him, she asked "if this looks like your Ilbrahim." His reply, "He will never look otherwise to me," suggests his unqualified pleasure in the artist's vision as well as in the artist herself. He dedicated to Sophia the special edition of this story printed in December 1838, warmly praising the drawing engraved as the frontispiece: "However feeble the creative power which produced the character of Ilbrahim, it has wrought an influence upon another mind, and has thus given to imaginative life a creation of deep and pure beauty." Courteously subordinating his own creative achievement to Sophia's, he assured readers that her drawing had won "the warm recommendation of the first painter in America" (obviously Washington Allston), then modestly asserted that whatever beauty and pathos the writer "could not shadow forth in language, has been caught and embodied in the few and simple lines of the sketch" (T-tT, p. 568).

He must have taken to heart Sophia's efforts to have the engraver respect those "few and simple lines." When the pamphlet version of the story first appeared, she told her father (in January 1839), the engraver Joseph Andrews returned the original drawing, but when "[I] compared it with the engraving, my heart sunk—for it seemed to me it was *utterly* unlike.... He changed the position of the eyes of Ilbrahim—darkened the brows—turned the corners of the mouth down instead of the original curve—enlarged the upper lip—& indicated the chin—which I had not—& did not wish to...." Andrews, however, made the changes she requested, and the engraving appeared in its second state in copies of *The Gentle Boy* issued on February 23 and thereafter (T-tT, pp. 566-67). Repeatedly in later years, Sophia would be dissatisfied by engravings of her husband's face; but in this one instance, she imposed her vision on an engraver.[15]

It was after making the Ilbrahim drawing that Sophia "took" Hawthorne's likeness, an ideal drawing of the face she would observe and portray for the next twenty-four years.[16] To Sophia, Hawthorne always appeared beautiful in spirit as well as form, and he did not feel inclined to disagree. Within a year after the drawing she made in the Peabody parlor, Hawthorne requested another, perhaps the only time he requested a portrait of himself. He had recently taken lodgings with the George Hillards in Boston and wished "Sophia would make a sketch of me, here, in our own parlour." Although he never recorded such an event, Sophia did present him with two of her other paintings—copies of Lake Como landscapes. "Pictures have always been among the earthly possessions (and they are spiritual possessions too) which I most coveted," he told Sophia before they arrived in Boston. Then afterward, he took

"spiritual possession" by examining them in various lights, hyperbolically identifying Sophia with the pensive figure on a bridge in the Menaggio and himself with the "noble-looking cavalier" beside her. Here, self-mockery does not disguise his genuine delight: it was "my very self.... It is not my picture, but the very I." Clearly, Sophia encouraged and extended Hawthorne's implicit belief in the primacy of spiritual portraiture as compared to a mere "picture."

But as an amateur artist, her influence on her husband was more pervasive. She brought to her marriage a good eye, a well-trained hand, and wide-ranging acquaintance with art and artists. She was talented enough to sell her copies of other artists' paintings for fifty dollars each, and her portrait drawings pleased family and friends. During her girlhood as a semi-invalid, she had copied the work of the famous landscape painter Thomas Doughty while he worked at an easel beside her bed. Washington Allston not only praised her copy of one of his paintings but offered the rare tribute of inviting her to copy others. Another famous artist, Chester Harding (who painted her portrait), praised her copy of his Allston portrait and also her own portrait sketches. She later studied clay modeling with the prize-winning sculptor Shobal Vail Clevenger, then made a bas relief medallion of her dying brother George and a posthumous one of Ralph Waldo Emerson's brother Charles. At least one portrait bust was made for sale, a study of the blind and deaf-mute woman Laura Bridgman.[17]

As a bride, Sophia found new ways to apply her skills—for example, painting second hand furniture, notably her matrimonial bedstead with its copy of Guido's Aurora at the head and an allegorical drawing of Night at the foot. There were no "real" portraits on display at the Old Manse, but a wide range of ideal ones. The "grim little prints of Puritan ministers that hung around" the walls when the Hawthornes arrived were banished to the attic, replaced by a Raphael Madonna, Sophia's "two pleasant little pictures of the Lake of Como," her painting of Loch Lomond, and a favorite wedding present—a bust of Apollo.[18]

Hawthorne's interest in art developed under Sophia's tutelage and surveillance, though he was more interested in truth, Sophia in beauty. During their years abroad, he tried hard to become a connoisseur. At the Manchester Exhibition of Art, for example, he devoted an entire day to historical portraits but judged few either truthful or beautiful. The basis of his judgment remained what it had been in Salem; he condemned any portrait calculated to flatter the sitter or satisfy time-bound taste.[19] The portraits that challenged his imagination in England and Italy were those whose painters did not worry about lace or buttons, or try for flattery, but presented visages that hinted at mysterious inner turmoil. On these grounds he praised the portrait of Beatrice Cenci: "the painter has wrought it in a way more like magic than anything else I have ever known," he said (*FIN*, p. 92). Beatrice's face was at once quiet and incomprehensibly sad, "as if the picture had a life and consciousness of its own, and were resolved not to betray its secret of grief or guilt" (*FIN*, p. 520). It was exactly what he thought a portrait should be, as perplexing and fascinating as a living individual.

Portraits in Hawthorne's Fiction

In four of his short stories and two of his novels, Hawthorne drew on the Gothic device of portraits with magic properties, though not primarily (as in Gothic fiction) to generate terror. The device served his own purposes: exploring issues of character. No portraits in Hawthorne's fiction are simply aesthetic objects or mere records of physical appearance. Through them Hawthorne raised questions about the kinds of truth a work of art can capture and the kinds of influence it can exert. Typically, a portrait in Hawthorne's fiction embodies secrets that remain in some measure unintelligible to the artist, the viewer, and the sitter alike. To the extent that the energy of a portrait seems to emerge from some invisible realm and to the extent that it exerts an inexplicable influence, the portrait seems a form of witchcraft.

At once the earliest and the most complex of Hawthorne's stories about portraits is "The Prophetic Pictures" (1836).[20] The "pictures" of the title are central to both the plot and the themes: Hawthorne questions an artist's ability to understand his sitters' essential characters and also his responsibility for such knowledge. The unnamed painter of the story is a man cele-

brated for unusual learning, technical skill, and—most important—for his ability to paint "not merely a man's face and features, but his mind and heart" (*T-tT*, p. 167). Hawthorne suggests the artist's power may be preternatural: merely by painting an action, he may cause it. The story concentrates on the portraits he paints of a happy young couple about to be married. The faces on the canvas seem marvelously lifelike, but curiously, at the last moment, their expressions change. Walter looks unusually animated, and the gentle Elinor looks inexplicably gloomy. Even more ominous is the undescribed sketch that the artist shows Elinor: all the reader knows is that she seems terrified.

Through the artist, Hawthorne explores the moral dangers of prying into a person's "inmost soul" without the license of love, dangers he faced as a writer. At the climax, the painter returns as a detached observer to visit the people whose portraits he has created and comes upon the very scene his sketch has prophesied: Walter has gone mad and is trying to kill his wife. The story questions the artist's moral responsibilities, asking whether his dreadful visions serve as self-fullfilling prophesies, though it presents the alternative proposition that he can foresee catastrophe but can not prevent it.

Of the four stories involving pictures, this one comes closest to Hawthorne's personal experience: the artist and sitters are the main characters; portraits are painted and judged as vehicles of truth. The story predates the major portraits of Hawthorne himself, but its attitude would remain the one he brought to all of them: a portrait might capture the truth about an individual that direct observation missed. Thus, fourteen years after writing this story, Hawthorne could say that Thompson's portrait promised to be a good picture even though he could not yet discern its "likeness."

Two other stories in the group take a more romantic approach to art as an embodiment of ideal truth. The ivory miniature in "Sylph Etherege" (1837) is an ideal portrait of a man who never existed, presented to the delicate Sylph as the image of her fiancé Edgar Vaughan by the conniving and "unprepossessing" man himself.[21] "The beauty of the pictured countenance was almost too perfect to represent a human creature" (*S-I*, p. 114). But in a sense it is her portrait. Painted in accord with Sylph's exquisite fantasies, the miniature is in that sense her creation, her emanation. It is removed from ordinary experience, but so is she. When, at the climax of the story, the sardonic Vaughan offers himself as the reality, vengefully crushing the beautiful miniature of the "phantom lover," the fragile Sylph is destroyed along with it. Reading Hawthorne's story as a wistful comment on love and beauty too perfect for this world, we can better understand Hawthorne's delight with "S. A. P.—taking my likeness" just a year later: the ideal of love that he and Sophia cherished could survive the shock of reality.

The portrait of "Drowne's Wooden Image" (1844) is, like the ivory in "Sylph Etherege," beautiful; but its beauty is earthly rather than Platonic.[22] It is the portrait of a real human being, not an embodiment of fantasies. In Hawthorne's robust Pygmalion story, written in the early days of his marriage, a "mechanical" woodcarver who is commissioned to make a splendid figurehead creates a startlingly lovely woman. Inspired by a real woman's beauty, he "discovered" her figure latent in an oaken log. Like the artist of "The Prophetic Pictures," the carver is a creator, though only this once and not because he has access to someone else's inner life. It is Drowne's passion that gives "warmth and sensibility to the lifeless oak" until eventually "the face became alive" (*Mosses*, pp. 312–13). When the townspeople are startled by the presence of an exotic woman who looks like the statue come to life, only the great artist Copley can understand: the woman "first created the artist who afterwards created her image" (*Mosses*, p. 319). The story expands on Hawthorne's belief that the best art results from an engaged heart as well as mind; thus, recognizing the artists Thompson and Leutze as sympathetic individuals, he thought they might be empowered to shape his "very self."

"Edward Randolph's Portrait" (1838) is the most Gothic of the group, though Hawthorne drew one element of its plot directly from Sophia's experience.[23] The story presents the portrait in two quite separate relationships to time: as an artifact it is not permanently fixed but vulnerable, subject to change; yet as a portrait it captures the timeless truth about a particular individual and a class of men. The story centers on a time-darkened portrait like those that had dismayed

Hawthorne at the Essex Institute, and, like "The Prophetic Pictures," it concentrates on the unpleasant though unavoidable truths portraits can convey.

We learn from the start of the story that the dark portrait of Edward Randolph hanging in the Massachusetts Province House is traditionally associated with evil. Some think it is a portrait of the Devil, others that a demon inhabits its "void blackness." As the story develops, it interprets its own legends: evil inheres in a despot and therefore in his portrait. Because Randolph had oppressed the people of Massachusetts, they cursed him, and his ensuing misery made his face "too horrible to be looked upon" (*T-tT*, pp. 261–62). The portrait captures the result of a process, but in turn it affects the present. It is at once a warning against behavior like Randolph's and a prophecy.

In the story's present action, Alice Vane, the niece of the Massachusetts governor, is an artist who (like Sophia) knows how to clean old paintings. To dissuade her uncle from summoning British soldiers to restrain the colonial "rabble," Alice secretly cleans the blackened portrait, then veils it. At the climax of the story she removes the veil to reveal the "dark and evil shape" of a soul in torment, its frenzied expression "that of a wretch detected in some hideous guilt" (*T-tT*, p. 267). The Governor ignores the warning, but he dies years later with the same frenzied expression on his face. The painter of Randolph's portrait had accurately represented the torment of a powerful individual who suffered a people's curse.

In *The House of the Seven Gables* (1851), Hawthorne again focused on the portrait of a seventeenth-century New England tyrant. Hawthorne began writing the novel in September 1850, four months after his sittings for Cephas Thompson had prompted him to think about his earlier portraits and the kinds of truth portraits can embody. He had recently left Salem, infuriated by his dismissal from the Custom House. In his preface to *The Scarlet Letter,* he vented that fury while taking stock of his past; and now, in his second novel, he used fictional portraits to explore characters' relations to their immediate past and their ancestral heritage.

The House of the Seven Gables makes use of three different kinds of portraits—miniatures, daguerreotypes, and oil paintings.[24] The miniature is the only one with charm; it shows the aged Clifford in his happy youth, before being wrongly imprisoned for murder. As his maiden sister Hepzibah lifts it from its secret drawer, we learn that it was "done in Malbone's most perfect style, and representing a face worthy of no less delicate a pencil." (While inventing this scene, Hawthorne might have remembered how much his unmarried sisters and widowed mother cherished the Osgood portrait: it comforted them in Hawthorne's absence, Louisa had said.)

The physiognomy of the young man in the silk dressing gown defines Clifford's character: his "full, tender lips, and beautiful eyes ... seem to indicate not so much capacity of thought, as gentle and voluptuous emotion" (HSG, pp. 31–32). Clifford's young cousin Phoebe later comments on the sweetness of the face, "almost too soft and gentle for a man's" (HSG, p. 92). The cherished miniature is a true image of Clifford even in his present debility. He is still sweet and gentle, and his pleasure at Phoebe's face and his pain at Hepzibah's prove him still a voluptuary.

If the miniature is associated with a leisured aristocracy that was dying out, the daguerreotypes in the novel are wholly products of a democratic present. The novel's young hero, Holgrave, is a daguerreotypist but also a writer who wants to tell the truth about the present and reveal the truth about the past. Through him, Hawthorne expressed his immediate knowledge of daguerreotypes and his reactions to them, as well as his own goals in this novel of sunshine and shadow, in which he felt free to "manage his atmospherical medium as to bring out or mellow the lights and deepen and enrich the shadows of the picture" (HSG, p. 1).

"I make pictures out of sunshine," Holgrave explains to Phoebe. Her reply is simplistic: "I don't much like pictures of that sort—they are so hard and stern; besides dodging away from the eye, and trying to escape altogether." Although she is right about the elusiveness of reflected images fixed on a mirrored surface, Holgrave corrects her assumption that all daguerreotypes appear "unamiable." Most of his portraits look that way "because the individuals are so. There is a wonderful insight in heaven's broad and simple sunshine." He even argues that the daguerreotype is su-

perior to a painting: "it actually brings out the secret character with a truth that no painter would ever venture upon, even could he detect it. There is at least no flattery in my humble line of art" (HSG, p.91).

As proof, he shows her a daguerreotype of a "hard, stern, relentless" face which she mistakes as his copy of an ancestral portrait of the family's stern progenitor, Colonel Pyncheon. Again Holgrave corrects her; it is a picture of Judge Jaffrey Pyncheon. The sun, however, has revealed that beneath his modern polish, he has the same grasping character as his ancestor. Hawthorne might have been recalling his own unflattering Whipple daguerreotype as he had Holgrave say, "Look at that eye! Would you like to be at its mercy? At that mouth! Could it ever smile?" (HSG, p. 92). When, near the end of the novel, Holgrave shows Phoebe a second daguerreotype of the same man, she immediately understands the image: "This is death!" (HSG, p. 302). She has learned that daguerreotypes tell no lies.

But the story establishes that Holgrave was wrong to think that no painter would portray an unpleasant character. The portrait of Colonel Pyncheon which dominates the Pyncheon house and the entire novel is symbolic of his evil influence on his descendants. Like the painting in "Edward Randolph's Portrait," this portrait has changed in the course of time, though its changes serve to accentuate its changeless aspect. The Colonel's sword had been, from the start, more prominent than his Bible, and, with the passing years, "the bold, hard, and at the same time, indirect character of the man seemed to be brought out in a kind of spiritual relief." Like those in "The Prophetic Pictures" and "Edward Randolph's Portrait," the Colonel's portrait reflects "the unlovely truth of a human soul" (HSG, pp. 58–59). Only at the end of the novel does the portrait lose its malevolent power; it literally falls on its face. Hawthorne's remark in his notebook a few months earlier that "there is no such thing as a true portrait" might be taken as a self-protective stratagem, since it is so completely at odds with the statements of the fiction. There portraits tell the truth, and the truth is usually sorrowful.

In his last completed novel, The Marble Faun (1860), Hawthorne used portraits to display character in more complex ways than ever before.[25] He had dutifully visited museums and galleries throughout his stay in Italy in 1858 and 1859, provoked to broad speculations about the kinds of truth latent or manifest in art. At once a connoisseur and a skeptic, he approached every portrait as a collaboration involving an artist, a sitter, and a viewer. He freely entered artists' studios as a friend, watched painters and sculptors at work, discussed their goals and methods with them, and judged their finished works for himself. In *The Marble Faun*—published in England as *Transformation*—he brought together his entire concatenation of experience and speculation. Transformation is always an issue with the portraits in Hawthorne's fiction, whether the emergence of a likeness, the deterioration of a canvas, or the effect of a painting on those who view it. But in *The Marble Faun*, the exploration of relationships between portraits and people is intensified. Here, four portraits—three of them fictional—serve to define character: Miriam's self-portrait, Kenyon's two busts of Donatello, and the actual portrait of Beatrice Cenci.

Hawthorne describes Miriam's self-portrait at length. In it, passion is fused with insight—it is the portrait of a woman "so beautiful, that she seemed to get into your consciousness and memory, and could never afterwards be shut out, but haunted your dreams." Donatello admires "the intimate results of her heart-knowledge," though he finds it "sadder than I thought at first" (*MF*, pp. 47–49). Then he begins to share in that sadness.

After the murder of Miriam's villainous model, the once-innocent Donatello becomes Kenyon's subject for a clay sketch and a marble bust. Hawthorne had described Donatello as Praxiteles' Marble Faun come to life; and Kenyon's clay comes to life as he tries to "catch the likeness and expression" of his sitter (*MF*, p. 228). But because his sympathy is limited and Donatello's character is in flux, Kenyon cannot shape the clay as "the index of the mind within." At one point "a distorted and violent look" appears on the work, which the remorseful Donatello accepts as his veritable image; but Hawthorne concludes the episode by describing a later "higher and sweeter expression" Kenyon accidentally touches onto the clay, a token of Donatello's true and eventual self (*MF*, pp. 270–74).

In describing Kenyon's unfinished marble bust of Donatello, Hawthorne continues to pursue issues of elusive likeness and hidden character. The image remains partly encrusted in marble, its features therefore not fully defined. It takes Hilda to explain to the sculptor why it should remain so: the incompleteness is a correlative for Donatello's incomplete moral development; it is an emblem of his transformation from a faun to a man. Here Hawthorne was making a point he often applied to his own portraits: truthfulness was dependent on the artist's insight and skill, but it was also subject to accident. An artist might attain a profundity he did not consciously intend.

Hawthorne made a similar point through his use of the portrait of Beatrice Cenci, an even more challenging image of moral identity than the busts of Donatello. For the novel's characters, as for its author, the portrait appears as a magical expression of the young girl's "unfathomable depth of sorrow" (*MF*, p. 64). If at different points in the novel Miriam's face and then Hilda's take on Beatrice's expression, it is because they share her problem of "grief or guilt." Thus, the portrait succeeds because it subtly intimates a hidden character with which others can identify. This is what Hawthorne did in his fictions and (as he occasionally granted) this is what painters, sculptors, and photographers attempted in their portraits of him.

The narrator of *The Marble Faun*, commenting on the durability of a marble portrait bust, says, "It bids us sadly measure the little, little time, during which our lineaments are likely to be of interest to any human being"; and he suggests that "it ought to make us shiver, the idea of leaving our features to be a dusty-white ghost among strangers of another generation" (*MF*, pp. 118–19). Some of the images of Hawthorne that have survived are, to use his words, "queer," some even "awful" or "horrible." Yet his lineaments continue to be of intense interest to many readers. Through these images made in the course of forty years, Hawthorne survives not as a "dusty-white ghost among strangers" but as an individual confronting friends.

The Portraits of Hawthorne

As a collection, the portraits of Nathaniel Hawthorne constitute a representative sample of the options for portraiture in nineteenth-century America. Miniatures, portrait sketches, and oil paintings were of course available throughout Hawthorne's lifetime. But, in 1825, when Hawthorne graduated from Bowdoin College, the only kind of image that was at once inexpensive and readily mass produced was the silhouette. By the middle of the century, an American tourist in Rome might commission a marble portrait bust, while at the same time, photography was expanding the possibilities for inexpensive portraiture. After the invention of the daguerreotype in 1839, any individual on either side of the Atlantic could preserve a detailed likeness in the "mirror with a memory." The many photographs of Hawthorne taken during his last years are at once evidence of his fame and of the rapid development of portrait photography following the introduction of the multilens camera and the wet plate negative, and the subsequent popularization of cartes de visite. Once the photograph made from a negative became widely available in the 1850s, portraits could be produced quickly, inexpensively, and in countless copies. Another technological development also contributed to the dissemination of Hawthorne's image. Wood engravings, locked into forms with type and inked simultaneously, could be reproduced quickly and inexpensively. Thus, from 1851 on, Hawthorne's engraved image was not only bound into books but also disseminated through weekly and monthly magazines.

Information about the artists who portrayed Hawthorne increases our knowledge both of nineteenth-century portraiture and of Hawthorne's expanding reputation. The first oil painting of Hawthorne was by the most famous portraitist in Salem, the second by a well-established Boston painter, and the next two by nationally celebrated artists—Healy, whose portrait was commissioned by President-elect Pierce and displayed in the White House, and Leutze, who had returned to America to paint a mural for the House of Representatives. A similar point can be established through the photographs of Hawthorne. He sat in the most celebrated studios of the time: in London, he sat for Mayall; in Washington, for Mathew Brady; and he sat in all three of Boston's most famous studios—those of John A. Whipple, Silsbee and Case, and James Wallace Black. Some of America's best draftsmen produced portraits of him, whether "originals," such as the drawing

by Eastman Johnson, or mass produced images such as Schoff's engravings for *Nathaniel Hawthorne and His Wife* or the magazine engravings of Thomas Johnson and Timothy Cole. Hawthorne's many posthumous portraits offer their own testimony, ranging from a cartoon in *Life* of 1884 (where Hawthorne and Emerson represent the New England literary establishment) to a statue on Hawthorne Boulevard in Salem, a bust on the portico of the Library of Congress, and a bust in the Hall of Fame.

In their number as well as their quality, the portraits of Hawthorne are impressive. The avowedly modest author posed for over four dozen portraits, including a silhouette, several miniatures, two crayon drawings, a number of daguerreotypes, numerous pencil sketches, four oil paintings, at least one marble bust, one marble bas relief, and over two dozen photographs. Most of these have survived. Hawthorne often wondered whether a true portrait could ever be made, and it is true that several of his portraits (Lander's in particular) seem imperfect likenesses. But at the same time he believed that even an imperfect likeness could suggest underlying truths. Given his personal reserve, it is disappointing but not surprising that he never speculated about what was revealed in his own portrayals. In fact, he had surprisingly little to say about any of them, and what little he did say was usually tinged with skepticism about their "likeness" and his own role as observer of himself.

The sittings he reported on most fully were arranged at the request of the fashionable portrait painter Cephas Thompson at the beginning of May 1850, six weeks after the publication of *The Scarlet Letter*. While Sophia and the children were staying with relatives in Boston, Hawthorne himself was staying in a rooming house, paying attention to the unfamiliar scenes and activities he encountered, including those of Thompson's studio. Although he said nothing about the first sitting, he commented at length on the second, his tone meditative and detached, though the subject was his own emerging image. He began by observing the results of the first sitting: "The portrait looked dimly out from the canvass, as from a cloud, with something that I could recognize as my outline; but no strong resemblance as yet." The "as yet" suggests that he expected Thompson to capture the resemblance, but his comment about three earlier portrayals indicates he had his doubts. None of the three had been satisfactory "to those most familiar with my phiz," he recalled, and then he ventured a pessimistic generalization: "there is no such thing as a true portrait; they are all delusions; and I never saw any two alike, nor, hardly, any two that I could recognize, merely by the portraits themselves, as being of the same man. A bust has more reality." Nevertheless he felt certain that Thompson was "a man of thought" with "truth in himself." He had painted a good portrait of Bryant, so Hawthorne anticipated a good one of himself (AN, p. 491).

He had "no assurance, as yet, of the likeness," even after his third sitting—a brief one because the light was inadequate—though he still believed "it will be a good picture." What he stressed this time was the studio itself and his own pleasures of sense and imagination as he sat surrounded by finished and unfinished paintings, inhaling the odor of paint and aware of a "mysterious charm" in the painter's equipment. Painting had always engaged his imagination, he said, "and I remember, before having my first portrait taken, there was a great bewitchery in the idea, as if it were a magic process." His grammar suggests the process no longer seemed bewitching, though (with a curious double negative) he confessed, "even now, it is not without interest for me" (AN, pp. 492–93).

Hawthorne's long account of his fourth sitting concentrates on the role of the painter and ends with a verbal portrait of Thompson himself. The beginning reaffirms his approval of this man who "seems to reverence his art, and to aim at truth in it." The painter's comments on the constraints of religious subjects were "suggestive," but even more suggestive was the discourse about "physiognomy and impressions of character—first impressions—and how apt they are to come right, in the face of the closest subsequent observation." By the climax of the sitting, Hawthorne completely identified with the artist. He perceived the exact moment when Thompson began painting with "more and more eagerness; casting quick, keen glances at me, and then making hasty touches on the picture, as if to secure with his brush what he had caught with his eye." Responding to the painter's excitement, Haw-

thorne recognized "the feeling that was in him, as akin to what I have experienced myself, in the glow of composition." But he noted with regret that Thompson then removed the portrait without displaying "what progress he had made, as he did the last time" (AN, pp. 497–99).

Hawthorne had nothing further to say about the portrait itself, though Sophia thought its expression was "illuminated," and he seconded her request to have the painting daguerreotyped. For at least two distinct reasons he liked the engraving of the portrait by Phillibrown: it was immediately recognizable, and it bore a "singular resemblance" to a miniature portrait of his father, who had died when Hawthorne was four years old. Although the image was bound into the 1851 *Twice-told Tales,* Hawthorne asked his publishers to include separate prints with presentation copies of *The House of the Seven Gables;* he wanted to be sure his friends as well as his family had copies.

About the "three portraits taken before this" which he recalled while sitting for Thompson, he had nothing to say except that those close to him had been dissatisfied with the "picture," the miniature, and the crayon sketch. Surely that was an exaggeration. Louisa reported that the oil portrait by Charles Osgood gave the family "great delight." The comment, nevertheless, presents Hawthorne's characteristic response: eagerness to see a portrait completed, then disappointment with the end product.

The pattern is evident in his comments about sitting for his bust by Louisa Lander, the only portrait mentioned in his notebooks except for the Thompson painting and two photographs. After his first sitting, in Rome in 1858, he caught a glimpse "of a heavybrowed physiognomy" that looked like what he saw in his mirror; and he made extensive comments about the artist, the studio, and the emerging image. He reported that the clay model delighted his wife and friends. But, for whatever reason, he later told Fields that the marble bust was "not worth sixpence," at the same time that he insisted on paying the price set by Lander. However justifiable his distaste, his children liked the bust well enough to preserve it and present it to the Concord Free Public Library.

It is an index of his open-mindedness and amiability,

as well as his sense of duty to his public, that misgivings about the Lander bust did not dissuade Hawthorne from sitting for another sculptor two years later, a German named Edward Kuntze who simply called on Hawthorne in London, bearing a letter of introduction. The portrait he made was a marble medallion, good enough to be displayed at the Royal Academy, to be praised by the *Art-Journal,* and to be purchased for Hawthorne by a group of his admirers, although Sophia said after his death that "loyalty to my husband seems to require it to be destroyed." Whether or not she did destroy it, the artist preserved his plaster version by presenting it to the New-York Historical Society.

Apart from the pencil sketch Sophia made during their courtship and the Phillibrown engraving, only one portrait seemed to give Hawthorne unqualified pleasure, at least in prospect and process. He was glad to have Emanuel Leutze paint his portrait, he told Fields, "which will be the best ever painted of the same unworthy subject." Because Leutze provided a fine cigar and excellent champagne for every sitting, Hawthorne was sure the portrait would have "an aspect of immortal jollity and well-to-doness." He guessed right. A half-smile can be detected in a few of the photographs, but the Leutze portrait is our closest visual approach to a jolly Hawthorne.

Of the over two dozen photographs of Hawthorne that have been preserved, giving detailed testimony about his public appearance and his fame, he mentioned only two in his notebooks, both group photographs taken in England—one in an Oxford garden in 1856 and the other at a civic ceremony in Liverpool in 1857. Even in letters to friends enclosing cartes de visite, he had little to say about them, though one comment is memorable as his clearest confession of vanity: his hair was not as white as the Brady picture made it appear, he insisted. Clearly, Hawthorne never enjoyed sitting for photographs during the last years of his life, the height of the fad for collecting cartes. He merely endured them, usually in a mood of compliant resignation. In such a mood in November 1863, within a year of his death, he mailed Fields a copy of the "grandfatherly" pose his friend had requested, though he felt "disgusted with all the undesirable likenesses as yet presented of me." He continued to play the game until the end, accommodating himself to the dissemination of imperfect likenesses in an imperfect world.

"The world is not likely to suffer for lack of my likeness," Hawthorne wrote to Fields on 1 April 1862, amused by his own willingness to sit for the Leutze portrait right after his photographic session at the Brady studio. Such amusement always had its serious side. In "The Prophetic Pictures," Hawthorne had explained, "It is the idea of duration—of earthly immortality—that gives such a mysterious interest to our own portraits" (*T-tT,* p. 173). The idea and the interest were always there.

After his death, his widow tried to persuade Fields to publish some images of Hawthorne and suppress others. Criticizing a photograph of him in a letter of 20 March 1866, she told Fields that Hawthorne was horrified at the idea of someone writing his biography, saying, "I wonder what his horror would be to see such a picture of himself. I dare say he would laugh—yet now he is not here to give the lie to such a falsehood, I should wish to suppress it at any cost." Fortunately, Sophia was not empowered to censor his portraits, though undoubtedly she did away with some. A dour or ugly portrait might well excite both horror and laughter; but the man who believed the sun does not lie, whatever tricks it might play, expected to find some degree of truth in any likeness, however imperfect. Taken together, these likenesses serve to delineate Hawthorne's life; taken in sequence, they provide a vivid record of how he appeared to his contemporaries.

This book provides a chronological discussion of all known life portraits of Hawthorne made between the time of his college graduation in 1825 and his death in 1864—paintings, drawings, sculptures, photographs, etchings, and engravings—together with comment on each artist and all available information about how the portrait was made, how it was received, and how it was exhibited or reproduced, all in the context of Hawthorne's responses to his own images and his attitudes about the kinds of truths such portrayals can provide. Some of these portraits have not been reproduced before—a bas relief, a miniature, and sketches by his family, for example—and a number of others (especially engravings and photographs) are very little known. It becomes possible to place many of these portraits in a line of descent; such families are identified and delineated. A number of portraits seem to have disappeared, including two miniatures, a marble bas relief, three daguerreotypes, and a stereograph, and these are so identified. Those images which are apocryphal, incorrectly identified as portraits of Hawthorne, are also identified.

The truest image of Hawthorne will always be in his writings. But in his time, as in ours, the reading public expected a visual image as well. This book presents the man of letters as he submitted himself to be seen in his time and suggests the way he saw himself.

Notes

1. Even his family and friends disagreed, though within a narrower range. Julian said his father's eyes were "dark blue" (*Nathaniel Hawthorne and His Wife*, 2 vols. [Boston: Osgood, 1884], I:121; hereafter referred to as *NHW*). Rose said they were "either light gray or a violet blue, according to his mood" (*Memories of Hawthorne* [Boston: Houghton Mifflin, 1897], p. 213; hereafter referred to as *Memories*). That their color was changeable is supported by Elizabeth Peabody's recollection of her first meeting with Hawthorne. She described his "wonderful eyes, like mountain lakes seeming to reflect the heavens." (Reported by Julian Hawthorne in a notebook published by Norman Holmes Pearson in "Elizabeth Peabody on Hawthorne," *Essex Institute Historical Collections*, 94 [1958]:264.) However, Hawthorne's Liverpool admirer Robert Hall rejected a phrase quoted by George Curtis in his commentary on Hawthorne's portraits in the July 1886 *Harper's*—"the well of thy dark cold eye"—and insisted the eyes were "very blue" (*Scrapbook* in the Berg Collection, New York Public Library).

2. *Memories*, p. 218. A catalogue issued by the London clothier Samuel Brothers in 1869 shows Hawthorne, Browning, Tennyson, Massey, Longfellow, and Tupper in appropriate authorial garb, with Hawthorne in a "Double Breasted Morning Suit" and carrying a top hat and cane. Reproduced in Derek Hudson, *Martin Tupper, His Rise and Fall* (London: Constable, 1949), p. 192.

3. *Hawthorne and His Circle* (New York: Harper, 1903), pp. 14–15; hereafter referred to as *HC*.

4. Letter of 23 January 1847. Unless otherwise noted, all Hawthorne's correspondence is quoted from texts established for the forthcoming Centenary Edition, Ohio State University Press.

5. *NHW*, I:233.

6. Ibid., p. 396.

7. Ibid., I:304. Sophia proudly described the gown to her mother: "I have made my husband a new writing-gown—one of those palm-leaf Moscow robes,—his old one being a honeycomb of holes. He looks regal in it. Purple and fine gold become him so much that I cannot bear to see him tattered and torn." A receipt from "John Earle & Co, Merchant Tailors" dated 23 March 1847 pasted onto page 7 of the Hawthorne family album owned by Manning Hawthorne lists items of clothing ordered the previous month: two vests (one silk), three pairs of pants, and a "Napoleon Coat," for a total of $42.25. Presumably these were the main items in Hawthorne's wardrobe for 1847.

8. Ibid., p. 309.

9. Ibid., p. 408.

10. Hawthorne mentioned the drawing by the English poet and novelist in his pocket diary for 21 July 1858: "In the forenoon, Miss Howarth came & sketched a crayon-portrait of me—for herself!" (*FIN*, p. 604).

11. Hawthorne was interested in the tenets of physiognomy at least as early as 1828, when he withdrew from the Salem Athenaeum all four volumes of a translation of Johann Lavater's *Physiognomy* (see Marion L. Kesselring, "Hawthorne's Reading, 1828–1850," *Bulletin of the New York Public Library*, 53[1949]:55–71, 121–38, 173–94). Although he was in general agreement with the physiognomists' argument that facial features offer valid indices of character, the precision of their schemes for analyzing, for example, the shape of the nose must have struck Hawthorne as absurd. Thus it is not surprising that the first edition of *The American Magazine* he edited in 1836 includes a parody proposal of a "science of noses" nor that he referred to Lavater's system in the following issue as one "utterly rejected" (pp. 268, 337). He did not utterly reject them himself, however. For example, the sensitive Ilbrahim in "The Gentle Boy" is described as "skilled in physiognomy," but he ignores his reading of the face of a treach-

erous friend. Further, Hawthorne used such details as a high brow or a weak chin to establish his characters, but essentially only as we currently use such indices, rather than as part of a detailed system. At some level he must have been aware of his own good looks and of the physiognomists' conviction that physical beauty was a concomitant of moral beauty.

12. *Hawthorne's Lost Notebook,* ed. Barbara S. Mouffe (University Park, Pa.: University of Pennsylvania Press, 1978), pp. 41–43. The corresponding passages in *The American Notebooks,* pp. 154–55, have minor differences of punctuation and wording. Many of the portraits Hawthorne regarded with contempt are of considerable interest to art historians, particularly the painting of William Pepperell by John Smibert and two portraits attributed to Peter Lely—Oliver Cromwell and John Leverett.

13. *Lost Notebook,* p. 11.

14. Ibid., pp. 28, 86, 77, 79, 80.

15. A note Hawthorne entered in 1838 reads, "Being dissatisfied with the position of Ilbrahim's foot, in her illustration of the Gentle Boy, Sophia said, 'She could not sleep because Ilbrahim kicked her'" (*Lost Notebook,* p. 79). Joseph Andrews (1805–1865) became one of the country's outstanding line engravers, best known for his portraits. He had studied abroad in 1835 and would return in 1840 and 1853 but spent the rest of his career in Boston. One of his students was Stephen Alonzo Schoff, who did three etchings of Hawthorne for *Nathaniel Hawthorne and His Wife.*

16. Sophia's comments about the sketch are interpolated in the closing section of her Cuba Journal which she copied out for her "dear friend" on 6 December 1838, dedicating it to him. "When I was drawing you last evening," she said, "I was obliged first to observe your actual countenance before I could make it visible again." She could imagine its "ideal perfection, and this is truer than what passes before our careless glance when we think we reproduce it." Convinced that portraits can reproduce essential character if not "ideal perfection," she regretted not having sketched one of the Cubans she had described, "that you might see the lightening glance and firm, earnest mouth so indicative of a dominant spirit." Manuscript in the Clifton Waller Barrett Library of the University of Virginia. Hawthorne's comment is in the *Lost Notebook,* p. 80.

17. For Sophia's life-long interest in art, see Louise Hall Tharp, *The Peabody Sisters of Salem* (Boston: Little Brown, 1950), as well as the biographies by Julian and Rose Hawthorne, the manuscripts of Sophia's letters and journals in the Berg Collection and the Boston Public Library, and her *Notes in England and Italy* (New York: G. P. Putnam, 1869).

18. After her marriage, Sophia continued to make drawings and paintings as gifts, and she augmented the family income by selling lampshades decorated in the Flaxman style for five dollars each and firescreens for ten. Some projects were more elaborate. Her last completed painting was a time-consuming copy in oils of a work borrowed from Emerson, a monochrome version of a bas relief Endymion, which she put up for sale at a hundred dollars in Elizabeth's bookstore, but she and her husband were so fond of it that they were glad to retrieve it and eventually hang it in Hawthorne's study at the Wayside.

Clearly, Sophia's taste was essentially traditional, and she carefully nurtured herself and her family on long-established works of art. From early on, the household included copies of a Claude landscape and a Rosa forest, two Psyches, and an engraving of Raphael's *Transfiguration.* Sophia proudly reported to her mother on 4 April 1844, "Una observes all the busts and pictures, and Papa says he is going to publish her observations on art in one volume octavo next spring. She knows Endymion by name, and points to him if he is mentioned; and she talks a great deal about Michael Angelo's frescos of the Sibyls and Prophets, which are upon the walls of the dining-room. At the dinner-table she converses with Leonardo da Vinci's Madonna of the Bas Relief, which hangs over the fireplace" (*NHW,* I:279). A long letter to her mother on 23 June 1850 gives an inventory of the family's art objects in Lenox—including a copy of a relatively recent Crawford sculpture (NHW, I:367–71).

19. Hawthorne and his family spent six weeks at Manchester in the summer of 1857, when his term as American Consul at Liverpool was nearly over, chiefly to visit the extensive Exhibition. See *The English Notebooks,* pp. 546–65, and my article "'Getting a Taste for Pictures': Hawthorne at the Manchester Exhibition,"

Nathaniel Hawthorne Journal 1977, pp. 81–97.

20. For comments on the portraits in these four tales, see Neal Frank Doubleday, *Hawthorne's Early Tales: A Critical Study* (Durham, N.C.: Duke University Press, 1972); Millicent Bell, *Hawthorne's View of the Artist* (New York: State University of New York Press, 1962); and Lea Vozar Newman, *A Reader's Guide to the Short Stories of Nathaniel Hawthorne* (Boston: G. K. Hall, 1979). The story was first published anonymously in the fall of 1836 in *The Token and Atlantic Souvenir* for 1837 and was included in the first edition of *Twice-told Tales,* published in March 1837. Hawthorne's note to the story acknowledges its origin—an anecdote about Gilbert Stuart he had encountered in William Dunlap's *A History of the Rise and Progress of the Arts of Design in the United States.* Dunlap related the story of a Stuart portrait in which the sitter's brother discerned signs of incipient insanity.

21. The story was first published anonymously in the fall of 1837 in *The Token and Atlantic Souvenir* for 1838 and was first collected in *The Snow-Image* in December 1851.

22. The story was first published in *Godey's Magazine and Lady's Book* in July 1844, under Hawthorne's name, and it was included in *Mosses from an Old Manse* (1846).

23. The story first appeared in the *United States Magazine and Democratic Review,* 2 (July 1838), as the second of the "Tales of the Province House," with Hawthorne identified only as "the author of *Twice-told Tales*"; and it was first collected in the 1842 edition of *Twice-told Tales.*

24. Another portrait is mentioned in Holgrave's story of Alice Pyncheon to stress her beauty: the painting by a Venetian artist was said to be part of a nobleman's private collection.

25. Hawthorne's use of art in *The Marble Faun* has received critical attention in many studies—e.g. Jonathan Auerbach, "Executing the Model: Painting, Sculpture, and Romance-Writing in Hawthorne's *The Marble Faun,*" ELH, 47(1980):103–19; Louise K. Barnett, "American Novelists and the 'Portrait of Beatrice Cenci,'" *New England Quarterly,* 53(1980):168–83; Nina Baym, "*The Marble Faun:* Hawthorne's Elegy for Art," *New England Quarterly,* 44(1971):355–76; Paul L. Brodtkorb, Jr., "Art Allegory in *The Marble Faun,*" PMLA, 77(1962):254–67; and my own "Painting and Character in *The Marble Faun,*" ESQ, 21(1975):1–9.

Early American Portraits

"A daguerreotype likeness, do you mean?" asked
Phoebe...."I don't much like pictures of that sort—
they are so hard and stern; besides dodging away from
the eye, and trying to escape altogether. They are con-
scious of looking very unamiable, I suppose, and therefore hate to be seen."*

*"If, you would permit me," said the artist, looking at
Phoebe, "I should like to try whether the daguerreotype
can bring out disagreeable traits on a perfectly amiable
face. But there certainly is truth in what you have said.
Most of my likenesses do look unamiable; but the very
sufficient reason, I fancy, is, because the originals are
so. There is wonderful insight in heaven's broad and
simple sunshine. While we give credit only for depicting the merest surface, it actually brings out the secret
character with a truth that no painter would ever venture upon, even could he detect it. There is at least no
flattery in my humble line of art."*

(***The House of the Seven Gables***, p. 91)

Silhouette (1825?)

A small silhouette of Nathaniel Hawthorne as a member of the Bowdoin College class of 1825 exists as part
of a framed set that once belonged to his classmate
Charles Snell. The Snell set of thirty-six silhouettes—
each 4¼ x 3¾ inches—is one of several of Hawthorne's
class now owned by Bowdoin, but the only one that includes Hawthorne. All the other graduating seniors
signed their full names beneath their silhouettes, but
Hawthorne's is signed only "Hath." Despite these
anomalies, no one doubts that the signature and the image are authentic.[1]

Almost seventy years later, Horatio Bridge recalled

Silhouette, 1825(?). Included in Charles Snell's framed set of thirty-
six graduates, Bowdoin College class, 1825; separate copy owned by
Manning Hawthorne. Courtesy of Bowdoin College.

that he and Hawthorne had decided not to have their silhouettes cut for the "Class Golgotha," a story consistent with Hawthorne's predilection for nonconformity at Bowdoin.[2] At this time it was the custom for Bowdoin seniors to have their silhouettes cut by itinerant craftsmen and to give copies to one another (the college owns sets dating back to 1809 and continuing to 1829). But not everyone complied: not even the Snell set includes an image of Bridge or of Henry Wadsworth Longfellow's brother Stephen.[3]

It appears impossible to determine when Hawthorne's silhouette was cut. Arlin Turner interprets Hawthorne's comment in a letter to his sister Louisa on 4 May 1823, "I do not believe you can tell whose profile the enclosed is," as a clear reference to his own silhouette.[4] Hawthorne might have sent another copy to Snell in 1825, signing it as he often signed letters to friends—"Hath."—although it is also possible that the Snell profile was indeed cut around graduation time.

The silhouette's authenticity is established not only by the signature but by another copy, unsigned, and currently in the possession of Manning Hawthorne.[5] It was given to him many years ago by an uncle, who said it had "been in the family for generations." Even before Manning Hawthorne acquired it, however, a relative had told him that Hawthorne refused to have his silhouette cut along with the rest of the class. Consequently, Manning Hawthorne simply inscribed on the back of his copy, "Nathaniel Hawthorne silhouette supposedly made shortly before his graduation from Bowdoin College in 1825." Whatever its precise date and occasion, the high-browed, straight-nosed silhouette in the Snell set presents a simple but ingratiating image of Hawthorne as a stalwart undergraduate.

Notes

1. Richard Harwell, *Hawthorne and Longfellow: A Guide to an Exhibit* (Brunswick, Maine: Bowdoin College, 1966), p. 16.

2. Horatio Bridge, *Personal Recollections of Nathaniel Hawthorne* (New York: Harper, 1893), pp. 4–5.

3. Letter from Arthur Monke, Librarian of Bowdoin College, 26 April 1982. The last set of silhouettes that the college owns is for the Class of 1829. The first autograph album of seniors is for the Class of 1835, the first photograph album is for the Class of 1856, and the Bowdoin College *Bugle* for 1900 is the first to print photographs of the senior class. But as Monke comments, we cannot be sure when the exchange of silhouettes ended, when the exchange of autographs began, or when seniors first began to exchange photographs.

4. Arlin Turner, *Nathaniel Hawthorne* (New York: Oxford University Press, 1980), p. 403.

5. Letter from Manning Hawthorne, 3 February 1981.

Miniature (1836?)

A delicately painted miniature allegedly of young Nathaniel Hawthorne sporting a moustache is now known only through a black and white photograph of it. It is a bust portrait, 6 x 5 inches, showing the figure turned left but facing front, dressed in a black vest, coat, overcoat, and bow-tied stock, and a high-collared white shirt. The hair and facial conformations could well be Hawthorne's in his young manhood. Julian once wrote of his father's portraits, "The best, in my opinion, was an exquisitely wrought miniature of him at the age of thirty"[1] Possibly this is the one he meant.

Julian's memory was not wholly trustworthy, however, especially about dates. He later said that the miniature "was painted from life, about the year 1836." He also said it was "the only miniature ever made of my father."[2] Perhaps Julian did not know of a Southworth miniature prepared in 1841 or one by Peter Kramer over twenty years later; but he must have known of the one painted for Charlotte Cushman in 1852 (see p. 38).

The miniature Julian recalled might have been painted for Hawthorne's mother and sisters after Hawthorne's move to Boston in January 1836. Perhaps Hawthorne had such a painted image in mind when he wrote to Sophia before leaving for Brook Farm on 4 April 1841: "I would thou hadst my miniature to wear on thy bosom." And it might have been the same "exquisitely wrought miniature" that Hawthorne recalled while sitting for the Thompson portrait in 1850, when he noted, "I have had three portraits taken before this; a picture, a miniature, and a crayon-sketch; neither of them satisfactory to those most familiar

Miniature, 1836(?). Now known only through a photograph in the collection of C. E. Frazer Clark, Jr.

Pencil sketch by Sophia Peabody, 1838(?). In the Hawthorne family album, now owned by Manning Hawthorne.

with my phiz" (*AN*, p. 491)

According to Julian, he owned the miniature for years after his parents died. When it was offered for sale by the London bookseller Francis Edwards in November 1918, the catalogue described it as a "very fine Original Miniature Portrait, in colours, in gilt mount, glazed, enclosed in case," gave its date as *ca.* 1840, and noted, "The above portrait belonged to Julian Hawthorne, who presented it to a well-known literary celebrity in 1875." Julian, however, claimed the miniature was stolen from him (by a friend) in 1878 or 1879. In 1919, it was in the possession of the English publisher John Lane, who had it photographed, and a photographic copy is now in the possession of C. E. Frazer Clark, Jr.

Apart from the problems of Julian's untrustworthiness, authenticating this miniature is virtually impossible. To begin with, there is no record that Hawthorne ever wore a moustache before he went to Italy. It seems likely that even if he had sported one for only a short

time, he would have made some mention of it. Nevertheless, he might have had one. It is also possible that a miniature of Hawthorne painted in 1834 or 1836 might have been retouched at some later date, with a moustache added. Possibly, too, Julian might have been way off on his date: the miniature might be a miniature daguerreotype made by A. H. Southworth in 1841, and then colored, gilt-mounted, and enclosed in a case—again, possibly with a moustache added (see p. 22). Of course another possibility is that the miniature was not done from life but is an artist's conception of Hawthorne as a young man based upon his image in old age. And there is still another possibility: that the miniature is a portrait of somebody else.

Notes

1. *HC*, p. 312. A photograph of the miniature appeared in the *Literary Digest International Book Re-*

view, 1 (1923): 8, illustrating an article by Richard Le Gallienne, "Hawthorne As His Daughter Remembers Him," where it is identified as Hawthorne "From a miniature painting in the possession of Mr John Lane."

2. Letter from Julian Hawthorne to the American bibliophile Alexander S. Graham, dated 1903. C. E. Frazer Clark, Jr., in "A Lost Miniature of Hawthorne," *Nathaniel Hawthorne Journal 1976,* pp. 80–85, reproduces this letter, another from Julian to Graham dated 30 March 1919, and a third from the English publisher John Lane to Graham dated 2 May 1919, as well as Edwards's catalogue description and notation, and the photographic copy of the miniature, 3¾ x 3 inches.

Pencil Sketch by Sophia (1838)

On the evening of 5 December 1838, in the parlor of her family's home in Salem, Sophia Peabody made a pencil drawing of her suitor. "When I was drawing you last evening, I was obliged first to observe your actual countenance before I could make it visible again," she wrote the following day. "I had never beheld your face until I tried to produce it," she said, though she had known Hawthorne for over a year. She had to fix his face in her mind before she "could make it visible again," but it then became fixed forever: "Now I shall recognize it, I am certain, through all Eternity."[1] Hawthorne's undated journal entry expresses his delight in that certainty: "S. A. P.— taking my likeness, I said that such changes would come over my face, that she would not know me when we met again in Heaven. 'See if I dont!' said she, smiling. There was the most peculiar and beautiful humor in the point itself, and in her manner, that can be imagined."[2]

A delicate bust pencil drawing of Hawthorne in the family album inherited by Manning Hawthorne may well be the likeness they both had in mind.[3] It shows a head with a faint suggestion of a smile, facing half right and looking in that direction. The long lashes and full lips seem almost feminine; but the high forehead, curling hair, well-defined eyebrows, straight nose, firm chin, and shell-shaped ear are all compatible with portraits of an older Hawthorne. It is almost impossible to determine what the figure is wearing, though he seems to be wearing his usual jacket and stock. Sophia wanted to capture her suitor's face in all its essential beauty, and

clothing had nothing to do with it.

Over two years after her husband's death, on 15 August 1866, Sophia explained to Fields why she felt entitled to criticize the right eye on one of Hawthorne's photographs: "Because I have not only looked at him as a model, for twenty four years, but I have so often tried to draw him which is is [*sic*] the only true test of seeing correctly." Although Sophia probably destroyed most of those drawings, this early ideal likeness and a later partial profile (see p. 78) evidently passed the test.

Notes

1. Manuscript in Clifton Waller Barrett Library of the University of Virginia.
2. *Lost Notebook,* p. 80.
3. The drawing, about 3 inches high, is the only item on page 8 of the album. It is identified as "an attempt to draw Mr. Hawthorne, made by Mrs. Hawthorne in early married life, and not at all approved by her." A pencilled note identifies the writer as "Rose H.," and Buford Jones observes that the handwriting seems to be Rose's. The drawing might have been done around 1842, though the youthfulness of the image as well as the fact that it is the only one of Sophia's sketches of Hawthorne's face to be preserved argue that it was the likeness made in December 1838. Sophia's disapproval is consistent with her response to any attempt to capture Hawthorne's ideal beauty.

Oil Painting by Charles Osgood (1840)

Perhaps the best known and most beautiful oil portrait of Hawthorne is the earliest one, painted by Charles Osgood in 1840 and now hanging in the Essex Institute. The half-length portrait, 29¼ x 24¼ inches, shows Hawthorne looking right. He has light gray eyes and dark hair, and he is wearing a cloak, coat, waistcoat, a black bow-tied stock, and a white shirt with a high collar. It is not established who commissioned the portrait and paid for it, but possibly it was Hawthorne's uncle Robert Manning. Manning Hawthorne writes, "I suspect Robert Manning had it done, as it always hung on the wall in the house he built on Dearborn Street until Miss Manning's death. . . . She was Robert's daughter. It hung in the parlor at Dearborn Street, and as Miss Manning never changed anything in her life and kept everything, I imagine Robert hung it there and probably commissioned it. It seems an odd thing for him to have done (why not one of his own children?) but he paid for Hawthorne's college education and really supported him for years, so he must have been fond of him. . . . Robert married fairly late—after Hawthorne left college, I think, and Robert may have considered him as a son."[1] After the death of Rebecca Manning in 1933, her nephew Richard Clarke Manning presented the portrait to the Essex Institute.

A letter from Louisa Hawthorne to her brother on 10 May 1841, or shortly after Osgood finished the portrait, expresses the family's pleasure with it:

The portrait came home a fortnight ago, and gives great delight. Mother says it is perfect; and if she is satisfied with the likeness, it must be good. The color is a little too high, to be sure; but perhaps it is a modest blush at the compliments which are paid you to your face. Mrs. Cleveland says it is bewitching, and Miss Carlton says it wants only to speak. Elizabeth says it is excellent. It has an advantage over the original,—I can make it go with me where I choose! But good as it is, it does not by any means supply the place of the original. . . .[2]

The following month, while her brother was still at Brook Farm, Louisa reported, "Mother apostrophizes your picture because you do not come home."[3]

The artist, Charles Osgood (1809-1890), was Salem's leading portrait painter. He worked in New York in 1831, but returned to his native town a year later and remained there until his death. That the Essex Institute owns forty of his portraits is an index of his great productivity. This portrait's date—1840—suggests that Osgood must have done it during one or more of Hawthorne's visits to Salem near the end of his service at the Boston Custom House.

The portrait was relatively unknown for decades after Hawthorne's death. It was photographed for inclusion in an article on "The Boyhood of Hawthorne" by Elizabeth Manning—the wife of Hawthorne's cousin Richard—and it was published in *Wide Awake,* a children's magazine, in November 1891. (The author of the article mistakenly referred to it as the earliest portrait of Hawthorne.) When the art historian Charles Henry Hart tried to locate a copy of the Osgood portrait several years later, his Salem correspondent John Robinson discouraged the attempt. "The fact is, Mr. Manning being a cousin of Hawthorne's feels a sort of proprietorship in all things Hawthornic," Robinson wrote on 3 January 1898. "Mrs. Manning wrote an article on Hawthorne's boyhood in the 'Wide Awake' November 1891 and I think printed a copy of the picture but I am not sure." A few months later, Robinson reported he had spoken to Richard Manning about the Osgood photograph but was told it had already been done for the *Wide Awake* article, and "he did not care to have it done again and copies all over the country—that it was only for a money making purpose and he had no interest in it." But five years later Robinson managed to send Hart a print from the negative of the Osgood portrait. On 22 February 1903 he wrote:

Quite by accident, I found the man who made the negative for the publication of the article written by Mrs. Manning for one of the Lathrop publications. He wondered if he owned the negative and I told him that, of course, he must, as the publishers had certainly had all the use of it they wished—I got a print for the Essex Institute (one could not be had of the owners of the painting before), one for you and one for myself. As next year, July 11, 1904, is the 100th anniversary of Hawthorne's birth, I presume there will be a demand for these things.[4]

The commemorative pamphlet which the Essex Institute issued for that occasion—the Salem *Proceedings*—did indeed reproduce the photograph Robinson had secured of the Osgood painting.[5]

But apparently neither Hart nor Robinson was aware that a delicate bust etching based on the Osgood portrait had been published in 1884, the work of Stephen Alonzo Schoff (1818-1904). In Julian Hawthorne's preface to *Nathaniel Hawthorne and His Wife,* he thanked his cousin Richard Manning for allowing "the portrait of Hawthorne, in his possession, to be etched by Mr. Schoff." (The biography also includes Schoff's etchings of two late photographs of Hawthorne. See pp. 58 and 96.) Schoff had been apprenticed to the famous engraver Oliver Pel-

Oil painting by Charles Osgood, 1840. Courtesy of the Essex Institute (opposite).

Etching by Stephen Alonzo Schoff, 1884. Prepared for Julian Hawthorne's *Nathaniel Hawthorne and His Wife.*

ton (who in 1873 produced an engraving of Hawthorne for the *Eclectic* magazine; see p. 71), and he was well known for steel engravings and for etchings based on portraits and historical paintings. His etching of the Osgood portrait appears as the frontispiece to the second volume of Julian Hawthorne's biography; it was also issued as a separate print, and it was published in Caroline Ticknor's *Hawthorne and His Publisher* (1913) and in several subsequent Houghton Mifflin publications. A simplified and stylized variant sketch by Don Weeks appears in the *Nathaniel Hawthorne Journal 1971*. Copies of the recently cleaned Osgood portrait frequently appear in the form of postcards, imprints on souvenirs, and book illustrations. A copy of the Osgood in oils, made by Clive Edwards, was purchased by the Salem Athenaeum in 1930.

Notes

1. Letter from Manning Hawthorne, 27 April 1980. See Frederick A. Sharf, "Charles Osgood: The Life and Times of a Salem Portrait Painter," *Essex Institute Historical Collections,* 102(1966):203–12.

2. *NHW,* I:229–30.

3. Ibid., I:235.

4. Charles Henry Hart Papers. Hart (1847–1918), a lawyer who became an art critic and collector, published articles in *McClure's Magazine* on the "Life Portraits" of Andrew Jackson, Daniel Webster, George Washington, Henry Clay, and others. He told Julian that he planned a similar article on Hawthorne for *McClure's,* but perhaps Julian's objections deterred him. He did acquire a number of photographs of Hawthorne, however, as well as the drawing by Samuel Rowse.

5. *The Proceedings in Commemoration of the One Hundredth Anniversary of the Birth of National Hawthorne, Held at Salem, Massachusetts, June 23, 1904* (Salem: Essex Institute, 1904) reproduces twenty-two portraits of Hawthorne, most of them owned by the Institute or by Salem residents.

Daguerreotype Miniature by Southworth (1841)

On 30 May 1841, Sophia Peabody wrote to Nathaniel Hawthorne,

Darling Husband, last night I dreamed that I went to Southworth's to see thy miniature, and that it was frightful! I immediately exclaimed, "I do not like it at all." I was rejoiced that it was a dream. I have been to his room; but did not find him. Tomorrow I shall try again. How I wish it were finished that I might take it to Milton.[1]

The Hawthornes' wedding would not take place for another fourteen months, and presumably Sophia wanted the miniature to show to the close friends she was about to visit in Milton Hills, as well as to compensate for her prolonged separation from her fiancé. "Southworth's" was the new studio of the man who would become one of the country's outstanding daguerreotypists, Albert S. Southworth. After establishing a partnership with Joseph Pennell the previous year, Southworth opened his Boston gallery in 1841 under the name of A. S. Southworth & Company. According to Beaumont Newhall, "The dateline 'Boston' first appears in the ledger on June 3, 1841; cash receipts are recorded over the past three months for seventy-three miniatures at prices varying from $2.00 to $5.00 each."[2] Thus, Hawthorne would have been one of Southworth's first customers.

The miniature might have been of Hawthorne himself, though it could have been a copy of the Osgood portrait, which Hawthorne's mother and sisters did not receive until early May. When Hawthorne wrote Sophia on 4 April, shortly before leaving for Brook Farm, "I would thou hadst my miniature to wear on thy bosom," he might have had the Southworth miniature in mind— whether it had been contemplated, commissioned, or actually completed by that date.

Although daguerreotypes could be set in cases on the spot, the fact that Sophia had to wait for hers to be "finished" suggests more elaborate arrangements. Perhaps it was to be hand-colored, or (as Hawthorne's phrase "to wear on thy bosom" suggests) set in a locket. We do not know what became of the miniature, though conceivably it might be the item of indeterminate fate that Julian referred to as the "exquisite" miniature of his father as a young man (see p. 17).

Notes

1. I am grateful to James Mellow for calling this letter to my attention; it is in the Berg Collection of the New York Public Library.

2. *The Daguerreotype in America* (New York: Duell, Sloan and Pearce, 1961), p. 42. Hawthorne is mentioned as a Southworth customer in Robert Sobieszek and Odette M. Appel, *The Spirit of Fact: Daguerreotypes of Southworth and Hawes* (Boston: D.R. Godine, 1976), p. xxi. The firm became Southworth and Hawes after Joseph Pennell's retirement in 1845.

Crayon Drawing by Eastman Johnson (1846)

The drawing of Hawthorne that Henry Wadsworth Longfellow commissioned from Eastman Johnson in 1846 hangs now, as it did then, in Craigie House, Longfellow's Cambridge home. It is a framed oval portrait, crayon and chalk on tan wove paper, measuring 21 x 19 inches, showing Hawthorne with black hair and eyes and wearing a black coat and loose cravat and a white shirt with its collar folded down. The drawing has black, brown, and white chalk shadows and highlights. Hawthorne looks fuller jawed than in other portraits, and his hair looks bushier. His head is turned slightly left, and his gaze is directed at the viewer. The drawing was owned by the Longfellow family until 1912 and was then given to the Longfellow Trust. It is the only professional drawing that has been discovered which was made of Hawthorne during his lifetime.

Although Eastman Johnson (1824–1906) is best known for his genre paintings and oil portraits, his early fame resulted from his crayon portraits. In 1846, when Johnson was twenty-two and his fame as a portrait draftsman was rapidly growing, Longfellow persuaded him to move to Boston; then he commissioned a series of portraits of his family and friends—including Ralph Waldo Emerson, C. C. Felton, Charles Sumner, Charles and Ernest Longfellow, Anne Longfellow Pierce, and Mary Longfellow Greenleaf, as well as Hawthorne. All these portraits hang in Craigie House as they did throughout Longfellow's lifetime.

Johnson's procedure with the Hawthorne drawing, and all the others in the series, was to sketch in charcoal, then finish with hard crayon and chalk. He probably charged what his friend Samuel Rowse did at the time, about $25 per drawing. According to George Hall, another friend who was also a painter, Johnson worked rapidly and surely, rarely making corrections, never requiring more than two or three sittings in his studio in Amory Hall, Boston, and sometimes completing a drawing in a single day. A letter from Longfellow to Emerson dated 25 November 1846 fixes the period of the Hawthorne drawing. Longfellow urged, "When you are next in Boston, pray take the trouble to step into Johnson's room and see the portrait he is making of Hawthorne for me."[1]

For whatever reason, Johnson apparently took longer than usual to complete Hawthorne's portrait. The first sitting took place sometime after 14 October, the date Hawthorne wrote to tell Longfellow of his readiness to have the portrait done and of Sophia's approval: "If you will speak to Mr. Johnson, I will call on him the next time I visit Boston, and make arrangements about the portrait. My wife is much delighted with the idea—

Crayon drawing by Eastman Johnson, 1846. Courtesy of the Long-fellow National Historic Site.

all previous attempts at my 'lineaments divine' having resulted unsuccessfully." The sessions with Johnson were long, Sophia wrote to her mother in a letter of 12 and 13 November, but the last sitting had been scheduled for 13 November.[2] Over four months later, however, the drawing apparently was still not completed. On Saturday, 20 March 1847, telling Sophia that he planned to travel from Salem to Boston the following Monday morning, Hawthorne remarked, "It is no matter about the session at Johnson's; but if thou choosest to give him notice, so be it." That he was not eager for the scheduled session seems clear from his postscript: "I shall probably go to Johnson's immediately after my arrival, before coming to West-Street. I hope he will be otherwised engaged."

Perhaps Sophia was "delighted with the idea" of a professional crayon portrait of her husband because she "so often tried to draw him" herself. Not only did she encourage Hawthorne to sit for Johnson, but she welcomed the idea of having another reputable artist try his hand as well. Clearly, she thought her husband's appearance deserved to be a matter of record. On 17 November 1846, Sophia wrote her mother, "I wish you would tell Mr. Cheney that Mr. Hawthorne was never so handsome as now, and he must come directly and draw him."[3] "Mr. Cheney" was presumably Seth Wells Cheney (1810-1856), a crayon portraitist and engraver who studied with his brother John, worked abroad from 1837 to 1840, then settled in Boston to do crayon portraiture for several years before poor health intervened.[4] But there is no evidence that Cheney ever made the trip to Salem or tried to capture Hawthorne's "lineaments divine."

Johnson's drawing is reproduced in the *Outlook* for 1898, illustrating Edward Everett Hale's article on "James Russell Lowell and His Friends"; it is also reproduced in the Salem *Proceedings,* in Hilen's edition of Longfellow's letters, and in a number of biographical and critical studies of Hawthorne. But anyone familiar with Hawthorne's other portraits must agree with Longfellow that "Johnson's crayon does not do him justice."[5]

Notes

1. Patricia Hills, *Eastman Johnson* (New York: Clarkson N. Potter, 1972), pp. 8-10; Andrew Hilen, ed., *The Letters of Henry Wadsworth Longfellow,* 3 vols. (Cambridge, Mass.: Harvard University Press, 1966), III: 124. The photograph is reproduced through the courtesy of the National Park Service's Longfellow National Historical Site.

2. Letters from Sophia to her mother are in the Berg Collection.

3. *NHW,* I: 310.

4. Ednah D. Cheney, in *Memoir of John Cheney, Engraver* (Boston: Lee and Shepard, 1889), writes of the brothers' close association with other artists who portrayed Hawthorne, including Schoff; of their fame in Boston, particularly for their engravings of Allston's sketches; and of John's engraving portraits of prominent literary men, including Bryant and Longfellow.

5. Journal entry dated 14 February 1847, in Samuel Longfellow, ed., *Life of Henry Wadsworth Longfellow*, 3 vols. (Boston, Ticknor, 1886) II: 111.

Portrait Sketch by Charles Martin (1847?)

Early in 1847, Hawthorne agreed to sit for a full-length portrait sketch intended for publication in the form of a newspaper woodcut. On 23 January, Hawthorne wrote Longfellow,

I shall be in Boston on some uncertain day, next week, and will call on Mr Martin, and arrange a sitting, either here or there. Since you do not shrink from the hazard of a newspaper wood-cut, I shall readily face it in my own person, though I never saw one that did not look like the devil. Full length, too!

On 19 January, Longfellow had written in his journal, "Martin came at noon and made a full length sketch of me for a newspaper. Very good. Kept him to dinner." And two weeks earlier, Longfellow had recorded three occasions when he "sat to Martin."[1] The artist was Charles Martin (1820–1896), son of John Martin, the celebrated English painter of apocalyptic landscapes. The younger Martin had recently made full-length portrait sketches of Charles Dickens and other English celebrities for the *Illustrated London News* and the *Pictorial Times,* and while visiting the United States during the years 1846 to 1853, he would sketch many American celebrities, including Washington Irving as well as Longfellow and perhaps Hawthorne, although this is uncertain.[2]

Despite his reservations about the "hazard" of a newspaper woodcut, Hawthorne evidently relished the idea of sitting for Martin, "here" in Salem or "there" in Boston. He liked being identified with his more famous friend as a literary celebrity, but in his letter to Longfellow, he professed concern about the appropriate attire for his portrait. The speculation is whimsical; yet at the same time it reveals serious concern about his public image:

I am puzzled what costume to adopt. A dressing gown would be the best, for an author;—but I cannot wear mine to Boston. I once possessed a blue woollen frock, which saw much service at Brook Farm and Concord, and in which I once went to Brighton to buy pigs. Gladly would I appear before men and angels in that garment; but on leaving the Manse, I bequeathed it to Ellery Channing. In a dress-coat, I should look like a tailor's pattern, (which certainly is not characteristic of my actual presence;)—so that I think I shall show myself in a common sack, with my stick in one hand and hat in the other.

Since he could not properly display himself in the garb he actually wore for writing, he decided to choose the less formal of the remaining two options.

In England on 15 September 1856, Hawthorne prepared letters of introduction for "the son of the celebrated artist," though it is not clear whether the son was Charles or his brother Leopold.[3] I cannot ascertain whether Charles Martin actually did sketch Hawthorne in 1847 or (if so) whether a wood engraving was prepared or published, nor have I determined what became of Martin's sketch of Longfellow. But given the artist's initiative and the sitter's willingness to face him, it seems likely that Martin prepared a full-length portrait sketch of Hawthorne, and it is at least possible that an engraved version may yet be found.

Notes

1. Manuscripts of Longfellow's journals are at the Houghton Library, Harvard University. On 2, 5, and 9 January, Longfellow sat "at Martin's." The entire series of events was initiated by his friend Charles Sumner, who had written, "Mr Charles Martin, son of *the* Martin, of Belshazzar's Feast, a young man of gay & pleasant address, wishes to secure a sketch of you for England, &, I believe, also for New York." Sumner invited Longfellow to "Call & see him—and look at me" while his own portrait was being finished. He told Longfellow that "Martin is connected with Yankee Doodle, also, I believe, with the Illustrated News of London" and, further, "He has done many of our 'first men.'" It is easy to understand why Longfellow was willing to sit for Martin, even though he noted in his journal for 2 January that the sketch of Sumner was "a doleful

thing." Probably similar praise of Martin from Longfellow persuaded Hawthorne to sit for him. I am grateful to Kathleen Catalano of Craigie House for sending me a copy of the Sumner letter.

2. I am indebted to Thomas Woodson for providing information about Martin's portrait sketches, gathered for notes to the Centenary edition of Hawthorne's letters.

3. I am grateful to Neal Smith for telling me about these letters, introductions to Hawthorne's good friend Evert A. Duyckinck and to Horatio Woodman, founder of the Saturday Club.

Daguerreotype by John A. Whipple (1848?)

The only known surviving daguerreotype of Nathaniel Hawthorne is the scratched half-plate, 4½ x 5 inches, owned by the Library of Congress and listed in their files as a work by Mathew Brady done between 1845 and 1853. Their copy negative of the daguerreotype yields a radically flawed reversed image which is nevertheless a recognizable half-length portrait of Hawthorne.[1] He is standing, turned half left but looking forward, wearing his usual black coat, waistcoat, and bowtied stock, and a white shirt with winged collar. His hair protrudes at the sides more raggedly than in most of his portraits, and his lower lip protrudes slightly more than usual. Several years after it was made, the daguerreotype was engraved for publication in *Ballou's* illustrated weekly magazine. Then, over thirty years later, a more accomplished engraving appeared in the *Century,* and a photograph of the daguerreotype subsequently appeared in the Salem *Proceedings.* Almost certainly, the original daguerreotype from which these later images derived was not produced in the Brady galleries of New York but in the Boston galleries of John Adams Whipple.

According to Leroy Bellamy, reference librarian at the Library of Congress, the photograph here reproduced is from "a half-plate, part of a collection transferred to the Library from the War College, originally having been purchased by the War College in 1874, when material from Brady's studio was sold for unpaid storage charges." Bellamy says "it is not possible to determine whether or not it is a copy, nor is there any

Daguerreotype by John Adams Whipple, 1848(?). Scratched half-plate, only surviving Hawthorne daguerreotype. Courtesy of the Library of Congress.

other information which could indicate why it is attributed to Brady."[2] We do know that Brady often copied other photographers' daguerreotypes of famous Americans. In 1912, Frederick Meserve intervened when he discovered employees in government archives discarding Brady daguerreotypes dating from 1845 to 1853, and, at his request, about sixty were copied on glass. It seems likely that the glass copy negative owned by the Library of Congress dates from Meserve's intervention.[3]

Louise Hall Tharp in her discussion of the Hawthornes during the winter of 1850 says that a daguerreotype of Hawthorne had recently been made, "probably at Fields's expense."[4] We do know that a miniature daguerreotype had previously been made by Southworth in 1841, and we know that Hawthorne's friend John L. O'Sullivan had suggested on 2 March 1845 that a new daguerreotype might be turned to advantage:

For the purpose of presenting you more advantageously, I have got Duyckinck to write an article about you in the April Democratic; and what is more, I want you to consent to sit for a daguerreotype, that I may take your head off in it. Or, if Sophia prefers, could not she make a drawing based on a daguerreotype? By manufacturing you thus into a Personage, I want to raise your mark higher in Polk's appreciation.[5]

The April *United States Magazine and Democratic Review* did include Duyckinck's article, though without an engraving of Hawthorne; but perhaps O'Sullivan's argument about the usefulness of a daguerreotype in the manufacture of a "Personage" helped persuade Hawthorne to sit for the Whipple daguerreotype. Possibly it also made him acquiesce when, in 1852, on a visit to Boston, "a daguerreotypist seized him, and took three pictures of him," as Sophia wrote her father on 4 July, "from which the man politely asks me to choose." She admitted somewhat grudgingly, "They are somewhat good."[6] These pictures do not seem to have survived.

The daguerreotype Tharp focuses on, however, did not seem at all good to either Nathaniel or Sophia Hawthorne. According to Tharp, Hawthorne's dismay about his haunted eye and protruding lip underlies Holgrave's comments about Judge Pyncheon's daguerreotype in *The House of the Seven Gables:* "Look at that eye! Would you like to be at its mercy? At that mouth! Could it ever smile?" Sophia laughingly comforted her husband with the assurance that his painted portraits captured his "true likeness," Tharp says, but "she would not let the daguerreotype be used for publicity and she rarely showed it to anyone."[7] The Library of Congress daguerreotype, with its relatively stern expression and protruding lower lip, may well be the one that displeased the Hawthornes, although the *Century* and the Salem *Proceedings* give its date as "about 1848."

An engraving based on that daguerreotype appeared in a Boston weekly, *Ballou's Pictorial Drawing-Room Companion,* on Saturday, 21 July 1855. It was the first publication of a Hawthorne engraving based on a daguerreotype, though not the first time an engraving of Hawthorne had appeared in the popular press: the Thompson portrait had been engraved for the *Boston Museum* over four years earlier. The relief form of

wood engravings had proved an economical and efficient mode of periodical illustration, since the blocks could be locked into forms with type and an entire page could be inked and printed at the same time. *Ballou's* "weekly literary melange" and the *Boston Museum* were only two of many illustrated weeklies available in Boston in the 1850s. *Ballou's* had begun life as *Gleason's Pictorial Drawing-Room Companion* in 1851, modeled on the *Illustrated London News,* and it was renamed after Maturin Ballou bought it in November 1854.[8] According to the editor, each issue of *Ballou's* was *"beautifully illustrated* with numerous accurate engravings, by eminent artists."

The engraving of Hawthorne, signed "Barry" and initialled "JB" in the block, appears in the upper middle of the fourth page of a sixteen-page issue. The engraving is framed on the sides and bottom by a brief but adulatory account of Hawthorne's career. The position on the page and in the issue are the usual ones for a feature on an illustrious contemporary, but it is unusual for such an account to begin with a comment on the engraving: "Mr. Barry has been successful in catching from the daguerreotype plate, the true character and expression of Mr. Hawthorne's head. It is the face of a scholar, a man of thought and refinement, and a poet. ..." Evidently, Barry worked from the daguerreotype itself, and because the artist was such a frequent contributor, *Ballou's* readers were expected to recognize his name. He was probably a member of a large family of Boston artists—perhaps Thomas J. Barry or David J. Barry, listed at the same address in the *Boston City Directories* of the period. The engraving itself presents a lively image of the half-figure, turned half to the right, as in later engravings and later copies of the photographed daguerreotype.

The Barry engraving is identified in *Ballou's* as "Nathaniel Hawthorne.—From a Daguerreotype by Whipple & Black." The noted photographers John Adams Whipple and James Wallace Black are listed in the *Boston City Directory* as partners from 1856 to 1859, although they had experimented together since 1852. From the early 1840s, John A. Whipple (1823–1891) was acclaimed for photographic experimentation (he patented both a daguerreotype vignetting device and the "crystallotype" process) and for the excellence of

Wood engraving by Barry, 1855. In *Ballou's Pictorial Drawing-Room Companion.*

Wood engraving, 1858. From the *Illustrated London News.*

the daguerreotypes produced in his studio at 96 Washington Street (between 1843 and 1845 in partnership with Albert Litch). He was one of three Americans to receive a medal at London's Great Exhibition of 1851 for a daguerreotype of the moon. The daguerreotype of Hawthorne made "about 1848" was almost certainly produced in Whipple's studio by Whipple himself. It is nevertheless provocative to see the name of Black associated with a Hawthorne photograph at this relatively early date: several photographs of Hawthorne would be taken years later, in the studio Black established after dissolving his partnership with Whipple, but Whipple himself deserves credit for the first photographic portrait of Hawthorne, and also for one of the last (see p. 94).[9]

Nearly three years after the Barry engraving appeared, on 20 March 1858, an unsigned three-inch bust engraving based on the daguerreotype appeared in the *Illustrated London News,* part of a series of brief illustrated commentaries on the careers of famous American writers, including Emerson and Lowell. The *News* essay on Hawthorne, evidently prepared five years earlier, begins by saying that "Nathaniel Hawthorne, the most popular novelist in America, is in his forty-ninth year," and announces that "he has been appointed to the lucrative post of Consul at Liverpool." A smaller but more elegant wood engraving based on the same image was issued in oval form, with the name Nathaniel Hawthorne printed at the bottom. An undated copy (source unidentified) is filed in the Prints Collection of the New York Public Library.

A much more detailed three-quarter length wood engraving of the daguerreotype was prepared as the frontispiece of the May 1886 edition of the *Century* by Thomas Johnson, the London-born artist who worked for both the *Century* and *Harper's* and who engraved two of Mayall's Hawthorne photographs for *Harper's* at around the same time. This three-quarter image is identified as being "after a daguerreotype taken

Wood engraving by Thomas Johnson, 1886. In the *Century*.

about 1848," and it was reprinted in two later issues of the *Century*.

Probably the closest approximation of the original daguerreotype is the photocopy in the Salem *Proceedings*, identified as "From the photograph of a daguerreotype, made about 1848, formerly in the possession of Dr. J. B. Holder, New York City." Angled lines in the background suggest damage to the original daguerreotype, but the face and particularly the eyes are much more closely defined than in the print made from the glass plate at the Library of Congress.

Notes

1. Harold Francis Pfister, in *Facing the Light: History of American Portrait Daguerreotypes* (Washington, D.C.: Smithsonian Institution Press, 1978), p. 149, says that the only daguerreotype of Hawthorne known to have survived is this one, in the Library of Congress collection, but asserts that it is so badly damaged as to be nearly unrecognizable. Removal of the cover glass of a daguerreotype for ease of copying was not uncommon, and the delicate surface was often damaged in the process.

2. Letter from Leroy Bellamy, 23 June 1980.

3. Dorothy Meserve Kunhardt and Philip B. Kunhardt, *Mathew Brady and His World* (Alexandria, Va: Time-Life, 1977), p. 29.

4. Tharp, *The Peabody Sisters of Salem*, p. 196.

5. *NHW*, I:284–85.

6. *Memories*, p. 195.

7. *The Peabody Sisters of Salem*, p. 196.

8. Frank Luther Mott, *History of American Magazines*, 5 vols. (Cambridge, Mass: Harvard University Press, 1930–1968) II:43–45, 409–12. Ballou owned and edited the weekly until 1859.

9. See Helmut and Alison Gernsheim, *The History of Photography* (New York: McGraw-Hill, 1969), pp. 128, 148. Whipple's advertisements in the *Boston City Directory* in the 1860s celebrated his achievements "from the small beginning in 1848" and his own reputation for "making the most perfect likenesses," which are also "gems of the Photographic Art." William Robinson, in *A Certain Slant of Light* (Boston: New York Graphic Society, 1980), pp. 30, 48, says Whipple won national fame and many awards for his innovative photographs, while Black was more the "artist." According to Pamela Hoyle, the two were in partnership from 1856 until Black left in 1860 to form a partnership with Perez M. Batchelder, which lasted until the end of 1861. See *The Development of Photography in Boston, 1840–1875* (Boston: The Boston Athenaeum, 1978), pp. 9–14 and *The Boston Ambience: An Exhibition of Nineteenth-Century Photographs* (Boston: The Boston Athenaeum, 1981), pp. 10–16.

Cephas Thompson Portrait (1850)

One of the best known portraits of Nathaniel Hawthorne is the oil painting by Cephas Giovanni Thompson, "painted for himself," as Hawthorne said. Hawthorne wrote more about sittings for this portrait than any other, and engravers copied it almost immediately: three came out within a year and others soon fol-

Oil painting by Cephas Thompson, 1850. Courtesy of the Grolier Club. Photographed by Charles V. Passela.

lowed. They would be the first Hawthorne portraits ever published.

The painting—30 x 24 inches, signed and dated in the lower right—shows Hawthorne as he approached the height of his fame, two months after *The Scarlet Letter* was published. He is wearing his customary black coat, waistcoat, bow-tied stock, and standing white collar. His eyes are gray-green, and his hair, apparently thinning at the crown, is combed back. He is seated with his body turned slightly to his right, but he is looking directly at the spectator.

Hawthorne had four sittings for the oil portrait in the first weeks of May 1850. It was apparently finished on 16 May, when he wrote his sister Louisa, "The portrait will be at the artist's (C. G. Thompson, 259 or 257 Washington St) after we leave town; as he has painted it for himself." He added, "Ticknor & Co. are going to have it engraved."[1]

Two years later, Ticknor bought the painting and gave it to the Hawthornes for their new Concord home. It was the only oil portrait of himself that Hawthorne ever owned. On 8 June 1852, he wrote Ticknor from the Wayside, "We are established here; and Mrs. Hawthorne will be ready to hang up the portrait, whenever you shall be kind enough to send it." It was in place by 4 July, when Sophia wrote her mother about a visit from General McNeil, one of Hawthorne's admirers. Leaving him to summon her husband, she returned to find "the old gentleman intently gazing at my husband's portrait."[2]

The portrait was put in storage when the Hawthornes went abroad in the summer of 1853, but it was returned to the sitting room of the Wayside from 1860 until the family left Concord in 1868. After Sophia's death in 1871, it was owned by Julian, who admired both the painting and the painter. He commented in 1903, "That portrait of my father..., which now hangs in my house, looks even better, as a painting, to-day than it did when it was fresh from his easel."[3] The collector Stephen Wakeman purchased it in 1908, and in 1913 presented it to the Grolier Club in New York, where it still hangs.[4]

From 1849 to 1852, Cephas Giovanni Thompson (1809–1888) maintained the Boston studio where he painted Hawthorne. He was already well known for landscapes and genre paintings as well as portraits, and many of his later portraits of American authors are in the collection of the New-York Historical Society. After leaving Boston, Thompson established a studio in Rome, and remained in Italy for seven years before returning to America. The Thompson family and the Hawthorne family became close friends during the Hawthornes' residence in Rome.

In his notebook for 14 February 1858, nearly eight years after their first meeting, Hawthorne wrote, "Mr. Thompson is a true artist, and whatever his pictures have of beauty comes from very far beneath the surface; and this, I suppose, is one great reason why he has but moderate success." On 11 March, Hawthorne offered higher praise: "I do not think there is a better painter than Mr. Thompson living,—among Americans at least, not one so earnest, faithful, and religious in his worship of art." Hawthorne thought Thompson had improved over the years, but the grounds of his praise— the truthfulness of Thompson's paintings, their beauty deriving from "far beneath the surface," and the painter himself as "earnest, faithful, and religious"—retrospectively comment on Thompson's portrait of Hawthorne, comments anticipated in the notebook entries made in the course of his sittings, when Hawthorne praised Thompson as "a man of thought" who "seems to reverence his art, and to aim at truth in it" (*FIN,* pp. 72, 128; see also pp. 10–12).

Lathrop describes the Thompson portrait in sympathetic detail, moving from relatively objective description to an impressionistic assessment of the sitter's appearance, mood, and character.

The face is smooth shaven and the cheeks are somewhat slender, making all the lines and features contribute to an effect of greater length and of more oval contour than that given by the later representations. The color is delicate; the large eyes look forth with peculiarly fascinating power from beneath a forehead of exceptional height and harmonious prominence. The hair is long, and recedes slightly on both sides of the forehead; a single lock in the middle curving over and dropping forward. There is less firmness about the lips than were characteristic of them in latter years; they close softly, yet even in their pictured repose they seem to be mobile and ready to quiver with response to some emotion still undefined but liable to make itself felt at any instant. In its surrounding of long hair, and of a collar rising above the jaws, with a large black tie wound about the throat in the manner of a stock but terminating in a large bow at the front, the beardless countenance is stamped with a sort of prevalent aspect of the period when it was painted, which gives it what we call the old-fashioned look. It is, none the less, a striking one; one that arrests the glance immediately, and holds it by a peculiar spell. There is no suggestion of a smile or of cheeriness about it; the eyes even look a little weary, as with too much meditation in the brain behind them; there is not a trace discernible of that sturdy, almost military, resoluteness so marked in the familiar crayon portrait by Rowse.... Here the face is pensive, timid, fresh and impressionable as that of some studious undergraduate unusually receptive of ideas, sentiments, and observations: it is, indeed, quiet and thoughtful to the verge of sadness.

Concluding his commentary, Lathrop reported that "Longfellow kept always in his study a black-and-white copy from this portrait, and in speaking of it and of the subject's extreme shyness, said that to converse with Hawthorne was like talking to a woman."[5]

The first known engraved portrait of Hawthorne was made from the Cephas Thompson oil painting in the winter of 1851, by Thomas Phillibrown, shortly after he came to this country from London. He arrived with a long-established reputation for line-engraved portraits, an arrival usually dated by the full-length portrait of Kossuth he engraved for Boston publishers that same year. Fields considered Phillibrown's delicate version of Hawthorne's head an "admirable likeness";[6] the entire Hawthorne family agreed, and Lathrop said it was "a steel engraving of considerable merit."[7] It was commissioned by Ticknor and Company, who published it as the frontispiece to their two-volume revised edition of *Twice-told Tales,* issued 8 March 1851. It exists in two states: as the engraving alone and with Hawthorne's script signature and "ENGRAVED BY T. PHILLIBROWN, FROM A PAINTING BY C. G. THOMPSON. Boston, Ticknor, Reed & Fields, 1851" beneath (*T-tT,* p. 559). It was republished in the firm's

Steel engraving by Thomas Phillibrown, 1851. First known engraved portrait, commissioned by Ticknor and Company for their expanded edition of *Twice-told Tales.* Prints given to Hawthorne's friends, including Melville. Widely copied.

1853 volume, *Homes of American Authors,* and in many subsequent books and periodicals.

Hawthorne had earlier accepted Fields's suggestion that the Thompson be engraved, but objected to the artist Fields originally proposed. His letter of 12 January 1851 responds to Fields's proposal that the portrait might be engraved by Jane E. Bentham, who had recently come to New York after completing engravings for the English edition of *Evangeline.* Hawthorne did not like Bentham's work but remained good-humored and even eager about the prospect of having his latest portrait engraved and published. He wrote to Fields, "Speaking of engravings, I should like much to see one of Thompson's picture. If it had been done sooner, it might have been prefixed to the Introduction to the Scarlet Letter; as being the very head that was cut off!" The 8 March publication date of *Twice-told Tales* indicates that Phillibrown must have made his engraving almost immediately after Hawthorne's comment.

On 22 February, after reading proofs for the April publication of *The House of the Seven Gables,* Hawthorne had written Fields asking that presentation copies of the novel be sent to about twenty-five friends, including "Mr. C. G. Thompson (the artist)," and said of the Phillibrown, "I presume you won't put the portrait into the [book]; it appears to me an improper accompaniment to a new work. Nevertheless, if it be ready, I should be glad to have each of these presentation copies accompanied by a copy of the engraving, put loosely between the leaves."[8] Perhaps Hawthorne did not object to inclusion of the engraving in *Twice-told Tales* since it was not a "new work," or perhaps he was not consulted.

Hawthorne reported his own response to the engraving and his family's initial reactions in a letter to Fields on 6 March 1851:

The package, with my five heads, arrived yesterday afternoon; and we are truly obliged to you for putting so many at our disposal. It is admirably done. The children recognized their venerable sire, with great delight. My wife complains somewhat of a want of cheerfulness in the face; and, to say the truth, it does appear to be afflicted with a bedevilled melancholy; but it will do all the better for the author of the Scarlet Letter.

Hawthorne then commented on a peculiar shock of recognition the engraving gave him: "In the expression there is a singular resemblance (which I do not remember in Thompson's picture) to a miniature of my father."

Sophia had registered her complaint "of a want of cheerfulness" in her journal that same day: "Mr. Ticknor sent five engraved heads of Mr. Hawthorne. The face is very melancholy," she said. In her own letter to Fields on 6 March, she began by praising Phillibrown's portrait but soon expressed her reservations about its likeness, or, indeed, the likeness in any portrait:

This is an exquisite engraving & looks just as Mr Hawthorne does, when in very melancholy meditation upon humanity; but the light is left out, with which his expression generally gilds all the mountain-tops of life. It is not so illuminated as the oil portrait. Yet of course I ought not to expect to be wholly satisfied with any but the real face, in all its variety. There can be one aspect in a picture certainly.

Nevertheless, she reported, "The children, Una & Julian, both recognized the engraving instantly." Her concluding sentences indicate she had made a real effort to appreciate the Phillibrown. "I just placed one of these prints in the window, & I find the resemblance is much increased by the lightening of the complexion, which is too dark in the engraving," she said, stipulating that "Mr. Hawthorne's hue is always pale, naturally, not pallid." A letter to her sister Elizabeth written that same day summarizes the same ambivalent response. The engraving "is very melancholy & contemplative, without the unfathomable sunshine, but it is him sometimes," Sophia reported, then echoed Hawthorne's comment to Fields: "it bears a wonderful resemblance to the sad reserved face of his father in the miniature." Two days later, she noted in her journal, "Mr. Tappan thinks Mr. Hawthorne's portrait looks like Tennyson." Perhaps the comparison increased her pleasure in the engraving.

Nearly a week later, Sophia recorded her pleasure in looking at the engraving in the company of five-year-old Julian. Hawthorne and Una had been on an overnight visit to Melville, and before Julian went outdoors to await their return, Sophia

took down the "Twice-Told-Tales" from the shelf, to look at the engraving. We enjoyed it very much. Blessed be Phillebrown, blessed be Ticknor, Reed & Fields, blessed be Thompson, C. G. Julian was struck with its life. "It is not a drawn papa," said he, "for it smiles at me, though he does not speak. It is a real papa!" Now that he has gone out, I have put it up before me, so that I can see it every time I lift my eyes.[9]

It is not clear why Sophia reached for the book rather than one of the separate "heads." Perhaps Hawthorne had put them aside or given them away. He had written his sister Elizabeth on 11 March that although he could not promise her an additional copy of *Twice-told-Tales*, since he received only six copies, "At any rate, I will bring you a proof copy of the portrait, which is finely engraved."[10]

Another copy went to Herman Melville. On a visit to New York at the end of May, he told Hawthorne, he "saw a portrait of N.H."—perhaps the Thompson portrait. And perhaps it was soon after that Sophia gave him the Phillibrown engraving which is now on display in the Melville Memorial Room of the Berkshire Athenaeum in Pittsfield. On the back is the handwritten inscription, "Herman Melville from Mrs. Hawthorne Pittsfield, Mass. 1851."[11]

But despite the pleasure Sophia took in the Phillibrown, she felt it lacked the "illuminated" expression of the original. When the Hawthornes first received the engraving, they had no way of knowing that Ticknor would send them Thompson's painting the following year; and Sophia felt compelled to request a more faithful copy. In her letter to Fields of 6 March, she asked, "Will you be kind enough, when you happen to see Mr. Thompson, to ask him to have a daguerreotype of his painting of Mr. Hawthorne taken for me? If you will do so, I shall be very much obliged to you." That her husband approved the idea is indicated by the postscript to his letter to Fields that same day: "Please to have the daguerreotype put down to my account, in your books."

There is no direct evidence that the daguerreotype was made, but possibly the "black-and-white" of the Thompson in Longfellow's possession derived from such an image. A small carte-sized bust version in the Clark collection (2¼ x 3¾ inches) might be a carte reduction from such a daguerreotype; the facial expression and contours seem closer to the original than to the early engravings. Inscriptions on the back of Clark's carte— "from Hawthorne's 'Our Old Home'" and the name "H. A. P. Carter"—point to still another derived image. Presumably, Henry Alpheus Peirce Carter (1837–1901), a Honolulu-born diplomat who was envoy to England and minister to the United States, owned the carte and had a special interest in Hawthorne's consular years. A bust engraving similar in proportion and tonalities to Clark's carte (though even smaller) appears on the title page of the edition of *Our Old Home* published by William Paterson in Edinburgh in 1884, as well as on the title page of other Hawthorne volumes issued by that firm.

The Hawthornes' relatively positive response to the Phillibrown steel engraving must be measured against their relative dislike of wood-engraved portraits. Hawthorne came to terms with them as a fact of periodical publication, but without expecting any of them to provide a good likeness. His letter to Fields of 6 March 1851 replies to inquiries about endorsing such portraits.

As regards wood engravings, I should not have the least objection, on my own part, to being diffused over the whole habitable globe in that guise; nor would I trouble myself at any sort of monstrosity to which my name might be affixed. If a man's face is to be cut in wood, he cannot reasonably expect to look like anything but a block-head. But my wife (who has the exclusive copyright of my physiognomy) is not quite so philosophical on this score.

Evidently Evert A. Duyckinck had asked Fields for permission to have a wood engraving of the portrait prepared for the *Dollar Magazine,* the illustrated monthly he and his brother George had taken over that month, and Hawthorne's response indicates that Fields had also transmitted other requests: Sophia "will consent, I believe, (though with much hesitation) to my being carbonadoed by Duyckinck; but I can prevail no further with her. Perhaps you had better refer the applicants to herself for an answer."

At least once before, Sophia had welcomed the prospect of her husband's portrait being engraved for publication in a periodical. On 20 April 1843, she told her mother, "Mr. Hawthorne received a letter from James Lowell this week, in which was a proposal from Mr. Poe that he should write for his new magazine, and also be engraved for the first number!"[12] Neither the proposal nor the magazine materialized, however, nor did an engraving proposed by another friend. In March 1845, John L. O'Sullivan, editor of the *Democratic Review,* wrote that an article by Duyckinck would appear "in the April Democratic," and O'Sullivan wanted Hawthorne "to sit for a daguerreotype, that I may take your head off in it. Or, if Sophia prefers, could she not make a drawing based on a daguerreotype?"[13] But for whatever reason, no "head" accompanied Duyckinck's commentary. We know that two years later, Hawthorne was willing to sit for a sketch by Charles Martin, which would subsequently be engraved, "though I never saw one that did not look like the devil" (see p. 25).

In the spring of 1851, however, no one was given permission to copy the Thompson portrait but the

Wood engraving from Samuel Wallin by Bobbett and Edmonds, 1851. In the *International Magazine of Literature, Art, and Science,* and two years later in the *National Magazine.* First image of Hawthorne published in a periodical.

Duyckincks. "I knew nothing of Griswold's intention to copy the portrait," Hawthorne told Evert Duyckinck on 27 April. "On the only occasion when reference was made to my wishes, as regarded the matter, I declined all such proposals, with a special exception as to the Dollar Magazine."

Griswold's dismaying "copy" appeared in the May issue of the *International Magazine of Literature, Art, and Science,* published in New York from July 1850 to April 1852. The engraving, 3½ inches high, occupies the upper half of page 156, preceding an unsigned review of *The House of the Seven Gables* by editor Rufus W. Griswold. The initials "SW" in the lower left of the block are those of Samuel Wallin, an artist who drew all the busts engraved for the *Illustrated American Biography* (1853–1855), all marked by his mannerism of curved lines.[14] The engravers "B & E" were the English-born Albert (or Alfred) Bobbett and Charles Edmonds, partners in New York from 1848 to 1854.

Nobody was more repelled by Wallin's "wooden effigy" in the *International Magazine* than Hawthorne himself. It is a "mangled head," he told Duyckinck, "a damnable phiz; a Peter-Grievous sort of a coxcomb, with a most intolerable air of looking his best." Hawthorne tried to console himself with the thought that the portrait was better than that of the journalist G. W. Kendall published in the same issue, but Sophia disagreed. "What is most provoking," he reported with rueful hyperbole, "the children both persist in recognizing the portrait, and will not be beaten out of the absurd notion that it is their father!"

Hawthorne was not alone in his opinion. Sophia referred to the "frightful woodcut" in her journal for 30 April 1851. Then two days later, in the *Salem Gazette,* the editor Caleb Foote commented ironically on the portrait of his friend, a "well engraved portrait of 'a nice young man,' whom we are very certain we never saw, and which is lettered, probably by some mistake, 'Nathaniel Hawthorne.'"[15] Probably Hawthorne had that portrait in mind when he asked Louisa, on 20 May, "Have you seen a horrible wood engraving of me, which, with as horrible a biography, has been circulating in the magazines and newspapers?"

The identical portrait was published in January 1853 in the *National Magazine,* a Methodist-sponsored eclectic monthly magazine which had begun publication the preceding July. Here the engraving occupies the upper half of page 17, preceding an unsigned article by the poet Richard Henry Stoddard, who had first met Hawthorne the previous summer. In his "Editor's Table" for the following month, Abel Stevens commented with pride about his magazine's commitment to faithful portraiture, intimating that all the portraits were commissioned by the *National:*

Our portraits are done by some of the best artists in New York; they are drawn by Walling and Oertel, and engraved by Orr and Kinnersley; the excellence of their execution is obvious to the most casual observer. In respect to their actual resemblance to the originals, we must remark that they are accurate copies of either daguerreotypes or accredited extant portraits. These we obtain from the friends of the originals, and use them on the responsibility of the former. Our artists are instructed to "follow copy." There has been but a single instance in which they have not succeeded well.

A second wood engraving of Hawthorne circulated widely in 1851, when he was especially newsworthy. On 6 September 1851 he "made" the first page of the weekly *Boston Museum,* "a literary chronicle of the times" published and edited that year by Charles A. V. Putnam. In a six-inch square at the upper left appears a four and one-half-inch wood engraving, probably based on the Phillibrown, signed in the block "J. W. Orr N. Y." and reproducing Hawthorne's script signature. John William Orr (1815–1887), born in Ireland but raised in the United States, was in high demand as a book and magazine illustrator by 1844, when, with his brother, he opened a major engraving plant in New York. By the time of the Hawthorne portrait, wood engraving had become "the principal reproductive medium through which art was brought before the greater public,"[16] and engravers' techniques were becoming increasingly refined. Yet by comparison with Phillibrown's steel engraving, Orr's engraving makes Hawthorne's features appear coarse, showing puffy cheeks, a bulbous nose, and empty eyes.

The wood engraving that Hawthorne agreed to let the Duyckincks commission would not appear until 1855; it accompanied the article on Hawthorne in their *Cyclopedia of American Literature,* published by Scribner. The Duyckincks had intended to use it for the *Dollar Magazine,* but publication ended with the issue of December 1851, before any article appeared that might warrant such a portrait. "Ethan Brand" had appeared in the May issue, but it was illustrated by an engraving of Darley's drawing of the climactic scene. Although the Duyckincks continued to publish the *Literary World* until 1853, that weekly never included illustrations. Thus, there was no occasion to use the engraving based on the Thompson portrait before 1855, no matter how good it was. Clearly it turned out

Wood engraving by John William Orr, 1851. In the *Boston Museum.*

better than the engravings of Wallin and Orr: it shows a meditative young man rather than a "coxcomb"; but the nose is longer than Hawthorne's, and the eyes are harder. The engraving, 2½ inches high, is signed "W. Roberts"—presumably William Roberts, a wood engraver who was born in New York around 1829 and was active there between 1848 and 1876. This image would have wide currency: the *Cyclopedia* went through numerous editions first in New York and then in Philadelphia.

Hawthorne would be "carbonadoed" again in this country and abroad, presumably without his permission. In England he encountered two more disagreeable wood engravings. At the railroad station in Chester, near the end of the Hawthornes' first year abroad, "Sophia saw a small edition of Twice-told Tales, forming a volume of the Cottage Library; and

Wood engraving, 1853. Frontispiece to Milner and Sowerby's pirated edition of selected *Twice-told Tales* and *Little Annie's Ramble and Other Tales*. The Hawthornes considered the portrait "queer."

opening it, there was the queerest imaginable portrait of myself—so very queer that we could not but buy it" (*EN,* p. 75). The edition, a piracy published in Halifax by Milner and Sowerby in 1853, included as frontispiece a wood-engraved bust based on the Thompson portrait. The very "queerness" of this portrait with its heavy chin merely amused Hawthorne, but three years later, another one annoyed him. Displayed in the Coventry market-place was "my Twice-told Tales with an awful portrait of myself as frontispiece" (*EN,* p. 579)— probably the pirated edition published in London by George Routledge in 1852, its "awful" frontispiece attributed to "C. Simms" (See *T-tT,* pp. 560–62).[17] On this occasion Hawthorne could not muster the philo-

sophical resignation implicit in his earlier observation that anyone whose face is cut in wood "cannot reasonably expect to look like anything but a blockhead."

Notes

1. I am grateful to Neal Smith for pointing out references to the Thompson portrait in Hawthorne's correspondence, including this postscript to Sophia's letter telling Louisa of the family's imminent departure from Salem.

2. *Memories,* p. 194.

3. *HC,* p. 262.

4. Presumably Sophia had the portrait with her in Dresden and London. I am grateful to Robert Nikirk, Librarian of the Grolier Club, who provided me with a copy of the portrait and information about the club's ownership. A color reproduction appears on the cover of the Club's *Descriptive Guide to the Exhibition Commemorating the Death of Nathaniel Hawthorne, 1804–1864* (1964).

5. George Parsons Lathrop, "Biographical Sketch of Nathaniel Hawthorne," in *The Complete Works of Nathaniel Hawthorne,* ed. George P. Lathrop, 12 vols. (Boston: Houghton Mifflin, 1887–1888), 12: 558–59. (Hereafter referred to as "Biographical Sketch.")

6. James T. Fields, *Yesterdays with Authors* (Boston: James R. Osgood, 1872), p. 57.

7. "Biographical Sketch," p. 559.

8. In a letter written from Lenox to his Salem friend Zachary Burchmore on 16 March 1851, Hawthorne said he had requested his publishers to send Burchmore eight copies of *The House of the Seven Gables* for distribution, adding, "I likewise requested the publishers to put a copy of the portrait into each of the books, although it is not intended to be sold with this work. If they should not do so, I will take some other method of sending you one." That Burchmore received the engraving is evident from Hawthorne's letter of 15 July. Sending regards to Mrs. Burchmore, he said, "I am greatly flattered by her hanging up my portrait."

9. *Memories,* p. 147.

10. *NHW,* I: 390.

11. Letter of 1 (?) June 1851, in *The Letters of Her-*

37

man Melville, ed. Merrell R. Davis and William H. Gilman (New Haven, Conn.: Yale University Press, 1960), p. 129. Melville might have seen the Thompson in the offices of the Duyckincks, since Hawthorne had agreed to let them prepare their own engraving for the *Dollar Magazine* (see text p. 35). Melville's Phillibrown was given to the Berkshire Athenaeum in 1952 by his granddaughter, Eleanor Melville Metcalf. Referring to Sophia's gift in *Herman Melville: Cycle and Epicycle* (Cambridge: Harvard University Press, 1953), p. 101, Mrs. Metcalf suggests it might have been presented during Melville's visit to Lenox on 12 March, or that Hawthorne might have taken it to Arrowhead when he and Una went there the following day. But if Melville owned the Phillibrown that early, and if the "portrait of N. H." he saw in New York at the end of May was the Thompson painting, it seems likely that he would have made some observation on the relationship of the two images.

After receiving her copy of *Twice-told Tales,* the English writer Mary Russell Mitford praised the Phillibrown engraving: "That portrait—what a head! .... It is well that a fine intellect should be fitly lodged; harmony is among the rarest," *Recollections of a Literary Life* (London: Bentley, 1852), p. 531.

12. *NHW,* I: 273. Poe had planned to join the staff of the *Stylus* as editor on 1 May and to publish a first issue that July, but as he wrote Lowell in June, the project "exploded." See Arthur H. Quinn, *Edgar Allan Poe* (New York: Appleton-Century, 1941), p. 384.

13. *NHW,* I: 284–85.

14. Frank Weitenkampf, *American Graphic Arts* (New York: Macmillan, 1924), pp. 183–84. Griswold would publish Hawthorne's "Feathertop" in February and March 1852.

15. I am grateful to Neal Smith and Thomas Woodson for the quotations from Sophia and Foote. Hawthorne's complaint to Louisa suggests that we may yet find copies of the Wallin published in other periodicals of May 1851.

16. Weitenkampf, p. 120.

17. A print of the Simms engraving is at the National Portrait Gallery in London. Several editions of Hawthorne's works later issued by the Edinburgh firm of William Paterson included on the title page a small oval engraving in a decorated border also based on the Thompson image. See C. E. Frazer Clark, Jr., *Nathaniel Hawthorne: A Descriptive Bibliography* (Pittsburgh: University of Pittsburgh Press, 1978), pp. 25, 33, 34, 37.

Miniature by Mrs. Daniel Steele (1852)

There is no doubt that America's leading actress, Charlotte Cushman, commissioned a miniature painting of Hawthorne in 1852, no doubt that he sat for it, and no doubt that it was completed; but we know nothing of the object itself. The request for a sitting came in a letter of 11 April 1852 from Cushman's close friend, the writer Grace Greenwood, who had been the Hawthornes' house guest the preceding December.[1] The Boston-born Cushman had been touring America from 1849 to 1852. She had decided to retire and live abroad and wanted portraits of some of her celebrated countrymen to take with her.[2]

On 17 April, Hawthorne agreed to her transmitted request, modestly telling Greenwood that he wished his fame had come earlier "so that my face might have been in request, while it had the grace of youth, at least." He promised he would "sit for Mrs. Steele,"— probably Mrs. Daniel Steele, a portrait painter and miniaturist who had worked in various southern and eastern cities for the past twenty years.[3] Evidently, Hawthorne had enjoyed seeing Cushman perform, and with courtesy amounting to gallantry, he said, "After the impression of her own face, which Miss Cushman has indelibly stamped on my remembrance, she has a right to do just what she pleases with mine. I am gratified that she wishes it."

Hawthorne might have had his commitment to sit for Mrs. Steele in mind when he wrote Franklin Pierce on 9 June 1852 that he planned to visit Boston the following day and stay until the end of the week, "being engaged to sit for a portrait,"[4] though possibly he was then planning to sit for the Healy portrait that Pierce had commissioned. Confirmation that he did indeed sit for Mrs. Steele comes from a letter Sophia wrote to her father in January 1854, telling of Cushman's overnight visit to Rock Park on 29 December and recalling that the summer before the family went abroad, Miss Cushman had requested her husband "to sit to a lady for his miniature, which she wished to take to England. Mr. Hawthorne could not refuse, though you can imagine his repugnance on every count. He went and did penance and was then introduced to Miss Cushman. He liked her for a very sensible person with perfectly simple manners."[5]

When Cushman sailed for England in July, she took along Hawthorne's portrait, as well as Longfellow's and Sumner's. Her relationship with the Hawthornes continued in Liverpool and developed in Rome, when they were all part of the same social circle.[6] But I find no record of the miniature itself—nothing about what it looked like nor what eventually became of it.

Notes

1. Grace Greenwood was the pseudonym of the popular journalist and travel writer Sarah Jane Clark. She stayed with Hawthorne and his family from 6 to 8 December 1851 and was among the friends who received complimentary copies of *The House of the Seven Gables* and *A Wonder Book,* though Hawthorne later criticized her writing as "miserable stuff." Greenwood was one of Cushman's traveling companions and house guests abroad.

2. Joseph Leach, *Bright Particular Star: The Life and Times of Charlotte Cushman* (New Haven, Conn.: Yale University Press, 1970), pp. 244–45. Cushman returned to America in June 1863.

3. According to George C. Groce and David A. Wallace (*The New-York Historical Society's Dictionary of Artists in America, 1564–1860* [New Haven, Conn.: Yale University Press, 1957]), probably the same painter who, as Mrs. D. S. Steele, advertised miniatures and portraits in Charleston in 1841 and in Richmond in 1842, exhibited in the National Academy with a New York address in 1843 and a Syracuse address in 1844, and as Mrs. A. Steele exhibited at the National Academy in New York in 1848.

4. See James Mellow, *Nathaniel Hawthorne in His Times* (Boston: Houghton Mifflin, 1980), p. 407.

5. *Memories,* p. 261.

6. See Leach, pp. 245, 249, 262–63, 287, 289, 312; and *FIN,* pp. 620, 623, 645, 652.

Oil Painting by George P. A. Healy (1852)

An oil painting of Nathaniel Hawthorne signed "G. P. A. Healy" and dated 1852, measuring 29½ x 24¼ inches, is owned by the New Hampshire Historical Society. Like the Osgood and Thompson paintings, it is a half-length portrait, showing the author wearing a black coat, waistcoat, bow-tied stock, and a white shirt with a standing collar. Hawthorne is turned half left but is looking toward the viewer.

This is the only Hawthorne portrait whose exact price we know. According to the Catalog of American Portraits of the National Portrait Gallery, Franklin Pierce commissioned the painting for $1,000 in 1852, the year of his presidential campaign, when Hawthorne wrote his campaign biography. After his inauguration, Pierce took the portrait to Washington and kept it on exhibit during his administration. It was inherited by his nephew Kirk D. Pierce of Hillsborough, New Hampshire, and in 1961, it was purchased from Kirk Pierce's daughters by the New Hampshire Historical Society.[1]

George Peter Alexander Healy (1813–1894) was one of the country's most successful portrait painters. Born in Boston, he studied there and also in France, where he attained international fame. In America from 1842 to 1867, he received numerous commissions to paint prominent statesmen and civic leaders, including Daniel Webster and Franklin Pierce, as well as Hawthorne. He returned to America for his last two years after twenty-five years of important commissions abroad. It seems wholly appropriate that in 1852 the President-elect would commission the accomplished Bostonian to paint his biographer and good friend Nathaniel Hawthorne, the novelist and consul-elect for Liverpool.

There are a few discrepancies about the date of the portrait, however. Although Healy dated it 1852 on the canvas, he was still working on it at the beginning of 1853. In a letter to Ticknor written from Concord on 21 January, Hawthorne wrote, "Could [you] ask Healy on what day it would be convenient to have me sit? I don't think Mrs. Hawthorne will be able to come again—she being quite ill of Influenza." Two days later, he reported that a cold prevented him from traveling, and asked, "Will you be kind enough to send word to Healey [*sic*], that he may not expect me in vain?" And

Oil painting by George P. A. Healy, 1852. Commissioned by President-elect Franklin Pierce and displayed in the White House. Courtesy of the New Hampshire Historical Society.

three weeks later, on 13 February, Sophia wrote to her father about the final sitting, on 9 February: "When I went to Boston the other day (Last Wednesday) I took the children, and Mr. Hawthorne had his last sitting." She reported the likeness "wonderful, and the whole style spirited and lifelike," although she had complained that Healy had not captured "the depth and sunniness of Hawthorne's eyes," he had "deepened" them in deference to this comment.[2] Perhaps Healy dated the portrait 1852 because that was when he began it, or simply because he failed to convert to the new year.

Other discrepancies may be attributed to Healy's lapse of memory over a period of decades. A letter he wrote in September 1885 to the Hawthorne afficionado, George Holden, does not in itself present a problem; Healy recalled painting Hawthorne in his studio on the corner of West and Washington Streets in Boston, though without dating the event: "I remarked to my wife after the 1st sitting, I never had a young lady sit to me who was half so timid as the great author whose work we so much admired.... As I became more acquainted with him his timidity wore off and he asked if Mrs. Healy would read one of Bulwer's works, which she did, he became very agreeable and talked freely.... He took great interest in the progress of the work and expressed himself highly pleased with the result." Healy then reminisced to Holden about his sitter's appearance: "He impressed me as a poetical Webster, complexion olive, the eyes rest in my mind as dark grey full of expression and intelligence." Recalling Sophia's presence at some of the sittings, he stated, "Mrs. Hawthorne approved of her husband's portrait and regretted that it was not for her instead of for General Pierce," and (perhaps conflating memories of Una and Julian) he recalled that "she had with her a fine little boy endowed with a quantity of curling red hair, whom I presume is the present gifted author." Healy concluded, "Soon after, Mr. Hawthorne went to Liverpool as Consul and I never saw him again...."[3]

Nine years later, however, in his *Reminiscences of a Portrait Painter,* Healy moved the date of painting Hawthorne back five years, though most of the other details in his account are compatible with his letter to Holden. "President Pierce, somewhere about 1847, requested me to paint a portrait of Hawthorne, who was a great friend of his," Healy wrote. "As I had vast admiration for Hawthorne's talent,—his genius one might say,—no commission could have given me more pleasure." Healy described Hawthorne's strong head, his timidity, and (as in the letter) reported the visits of his red-headed son. But the date of 1847 (when Julian would have been only two years old) is not the only anomaly. Healy was obviously mistaken in recalling "the novelist was then about forty years of age," although there is no reason to doubt his recollection that Hawthorne was "a most striking-looking man, after the fashion of Webster: heavy black eyebrows overshadowed the eyes...." Most puzzling is Healy's recollection that Hawthorne "had a shock of black hair and a heavy moustache."[4] The Healy portrait we know shows a clean-shaven Hawthorne, and, as far as we know, Hawthorne first grew a moustache years later in Italy.

Two more recent publications repeat the anomalous details of Healy's *Reminiscences.* The souvenir pamphlet of a 1950 exhibition of Healy's portraits repeats the report that Pierce asked Healy to paint Hawthorne in 1847, then quotes Healy's alleged comments to his wife about Hawthorne's shyness, "his heavy eyebrows, his shock of wavy dark hair and thick moustache."[5] A subsequent study of Healy by his granddaughter, Marie de Mare, adds to the confusion by assuming that there were two Hawthorne portraits, one done in 1847 and one in 1852. De Mare's account of an 1847 portrait repeats Healy's comments about Hawthorne's shyness and Mrs. Hawthorne's visits. But she then states, "In May, 1852, George and Louisa Healy arrived in Boston where the artist set at once to paint another portrait of Hawthorne in an easy, happy atmosphere very different from the first tense sittings of a few years ago." The crucial word, of course, is *another.*[6]

It is possible that there were two paintings, and although it seems unlikely, someone may yet find an 1847 portrait by Healy showing Hawthorne with a moustache.

Photographs of Healy's portrait have been published in the Salem *Proceedings* and other volumes; but of the four oil paintings made of Hawthorne during his lifetime, this is the only one that was never etched or engraved.

Notes

1. According to William Copeley, Associate Librarian of the New Hampshire Historical Society, Healy's portraits of Daniel Webster and Franklin Pierce were also purchased by the Society in 1961.

2. Sophia's letter is in the Berg Collection.

3. Letter in the collection of C. E. Frazer Clark, Jr. See Jane C. Giffen, "Three Healy Portraits," *Historical New Hampshire*, 20 (1965):32–36.

4. George P. A. Healy, *Reminiscences of a Portrait Painter* (Chicago: McClurg, 1894), pp. 210–13.

5. *A Souvenir of the Exhibition Entitled Healy's Sitters* (Richmond, Virginia: Museum of Fine Arts, 1950), p. 59.

6. Marie de Mare, *G. P. A. Healy, American Artist* (New York: David McKay, 1954), pp. 159–60, 173.

Portraits in England and Italy

"A marble bust...bids us sadly measure the little, little time, during which our lineaments are likely to be of interest to any human being....And it ought to make us shiver, the idea of leaving our features to be a dusty-white ghost among strangers of another generation...."
(The Marble Faun, pp. 118–19)

Oxford Group Photograph
by Philip Delamotte (1856)

On 30 August 1856, Nathaniel and Sophia Hawthorne and their good friend Francis Bennoch traveled to Oxford for a six-day visit with Richard James Spiers, "a very hospitable gentleman, an ex-Mayor of Oxford, and a friend of Bennoch and of the Halls." They spent agreeable days touring the colleges and such memorable places as Blenheim Palace; and on the day before their departure, in the course of a barge tour on the Thames, they "picked up Mr. De La Motte, a famous photographist" and two other artists. The next day, the "photographist...had breakfasted with us; and Mr. Spiers wished him to take a photograph of the whole party" (*EN*, pp. 399, 420, 422).

At that time, Philip Henry Delamotte (1820–1890), a professor of drawing at King's College, London, who also taught photography, was widely recognized as one of England's foremost photographers and photographic experimenters. His manual, *The Practice of Photography,* was published in 1853. And in 1855, 160 of his albumen prints of the reconstruction of the Crystal Palace and events celebrated there were published in a well-received volume entitled *Photographic Views of the Progress of the Crystal Palace, Sydenham.*[1] Thus, the task of photographing the Spiers's guests could not have seemed a formidable challenge.

Yet Delamotte did have to decide on the proper exposure time for his collodion plate in the morning light. "So," as Hawthorne noted, "in the first place, before the rest were assembled, he made an experimental group of such as were there; and I did not like my own aspect very much." The "experimental group" was apparently not preserved, but it is not unusual to find Hawthorne displeased by his own aspect.

His response to the photograph of the larger group was more complex:

Afterwards, when we were all come, he arranged us under a tree, in the garden—Mr. & Mrs. Spiers, with their eldest son, Mr. and Mrs. Hall, Fanny, Mr. Addison, my wife and me—and stained the glass with our figures and faces, in the twinkling of an eye; not my wife's face, however, for she turned it away, and left only a pattern of her bonnet and gown; and Mrs. Hall, too, refused to countenance the proceeding, otherwise than with her back. But all the rest of us were caught, to the life; and I was really a little startled at recognizing myself so apart from myself, and done so quickly too. (EN, p. 422)

Hawthorne was impressed by Delamotte's speed and the accuracy of the photographic image, but he was especially amazed at his own self-recognition. His comment recalls the "shape of mystery" attentively studied in "Monsieur du Miroir" and an even earlier notebook entry:

A perception, for a moment, of one's eventual and moral self, as if it were another person,—the observant faculty being separated, and looking intently at the qualities of the character. There is a surprise when this

43

Photograph by Philip Delamotte, 1856. One of two group portraits taken in an Oxford garden by one of England's foremost photographers. Courtesy of The Bancroft Library.

happens,—this getting out of one's self,—and then the observer sees how queer a fellow he is. (**AN**, *p. 178*)

It was probably the first time Hawthorne had been photographed since the daguerreotype "seized" from him four years earlier, and it was also probably his first participation in a group photograph and in an outdoor photograph. By contrast with early daguerreotypists, who usually required sitters to remain still for several minutes under carefully arranged conditions, Delamotte could fix an image in seconds, quickly adjusting to his sitters and the available light. Hawthorne was obviously delighted that a picture could be made "in the twinkling of an eye." Further, the image of Delamotte "staining" the glass suggests that the photographer let Hawthorne see the collodion plate (which would be taken back to the studio and used to generate paper prints). Probably, Hawthorne had never seen a negative before, almost certainly not his own negative image. This could readily account for his sense of displacement—his feeling "really a little startled at recognizing myself so apart from myself."

But he would have no trouble recognizing himself even in a negative, dressed in his familiar frock coat, vest, white high-collared shirt, and bow tie, standing with legs slightly apart, his eyes lowered as if in thought. And whether as a function of Delamotte's pose, his own posture, or both, he saw himself standing apart from the rest of the group, appearing wholly separable from them. That too was part of being "caught, to the life."

In his biography of his parents, Julian Hawthorne commented on the occasion and on the photograph.

One of the pleasantest excursions of the summer was to Oxford, where Hawthorne and his wife were very kindly received and entertained by Mr. Speirs [sic], the ex-mayor of the town. They remained several days, and before departing, the whole party (including Mr. and Mrs. S. C. Hall) were photographed on Mr. Speirs's [sic] lawn. In this photograph Hawthorne stands on the extreme right, facing the spectator, with his feet apart and his hands behind him, and his black frock coat unbuttoned. So far as figure and pose go, it is an admirable likeness; but the photograph **quâ** *photograph, is execrably bad, and the faces of none of the group are recognizable.*[2]

Julian was right about the admirable likeness but wrong about the recognizability of the group. Hawthorne's account facilitates the identification: Sophia Hawthorne is on the left, her face averted and obscured by her movement; Mrs. Spiers stands beside her holding a parasol, next to her son, whose arm is in a sling; next to him is Fanny, the adopted daughter of Mr. and Mrs. S. C. Hall, partly hidden by the Puseyite Mr. Addison; next comes Mr. Spiers; then Mrs. Hall, seated in front of her husband but concealing her countenance; and finally, Hawthorne himself stands at the far right.

The detail of Julian Hawthorne's description suggests that he wrote it soon after looking at the photograph. Indeed, he owned one of the two surviving prints (measuring 8¼ X 6½ inches, and mounted on a larger sheet). Presumably it was one Spiers sent Hawthorne shortly after the Oxford visit, and it is now part of the collection of Julian's papers at the Bancroft Library at Berkeley. The second surviving print was presumably retained by Spiers for himself. It was included in a volume of nineteenth-century photographs acquired by the Bodleian Library of Oxford University, marked

"Photographs by R. Phené Spiers"—perhaps the mayor's oldest son, Richard Spiers, Jr., who appears in the photograph with his arm in a sling.[3]

We can understand Julian's judgment that the photograph is "execrably bad": the individuals are awkwardly grouped, and Sophia literally has no face. But in context, the full-length photograph of Hawthorne appears all the more remarkable. For Hawthorne himself, it was a technological marvel and also a mode of self-confrontation. Never before or again did he describe in his journal the experience of being photographed. It was "the last important incident of our visit to Oxford."

Notes

1. Delamotte continued working as a professional photographer throughout his lifetime. See Gernsheim, pp. 176, 237, 267, 280. His manual went through three editions in four years and has recently been reprinted. Bennoch had already left Oxford when the Spiers photograph was taken.

2. *NHW,* II: 131.

3. Information about the Bodley's print is from Bruce Barker-Benfield, Assistant Librarian, in a letter to James Mellow of 9 December 1978. Penciled notes at the bottom of the print identify Fanny Hall and Mr. Addison and confirm Hawthorne's date of 4 September 1856. A penciled note above the Bancroft print, giving the date incorrectly, reads "A scene in the garden of the Mayor of Oxford during a visit we made there in 1855," and the names of all those in the group are penciled below. As is evident in the photocopy, Mrs. Hawthorne's head and hat are nearly obliterated by retouching in ink.

Liverpool Group Photograph (1857)

Nathaniel Hawthorne appears in his role as United States Consul to Liverpool in a faded sepia-colored group photograph taken at the laying of the foundation stone of the Liverpool Free Public Library on 15 April 1857. William Brown, donor of the library, is in the center of the picture with Hawthorne almost directly behind him, surrounded by a group of Liverpool notables. The *Liverpool Mercury* reported that two photographers commemorated the event, a Mr. Keith of Castle Street and a Mr. Berry, but there is no way of knowing which of them took this photograph.

Newspapers at the time did not reproduce photographs,[1] but an account of the proceedings at the library site and at the banquet that followed appeared in the *Liverpool Mercury* supplement for 17 April, and in the *Liverpool Mail* and the *Illustrated London News* the following day. An engraving of a photograph showing the cornerstone being laid was published in the *London Illustrated News* for 2 May, but none of the figures can be clearly identified as Hawthorne.

The ceremonies were memorable enough for Hawthorne to devote his entire notebook entry of 19 April to them, beginning with his arrival at the Town Hall (*EN,* pp. 457–60). He was "cordially greeted by Monckton Milnes, whom I like," and Milnes then introduced him to "a comely young man, in a brown frock, and pantaloons plaided of a very large pattern," who resembled "a salesman in a dry-goods establishment." He turned out to be Lord Stanley, a man of "gentle dignity," committed by his hereditary position to public service, despite such disabilities as a malformed mouth and "puffy" voice. Both these men appear in the surviving photograph, standing not far from Hawthorne.

Hawthorne next wrote of forming into procession with the other invited guests and marching four abreast through crowded streets, "a trail of ordinary-looking individuals, in great coats, and with precautionary umbrellas." An equivalent American procession, he commented, would have been more "picturesque."

He singled out only three individuals—"The only characteristic or professional costumes, as far as I noticed, was that of the Bishop of Chester, in his flat cap and black silk gown, and that of Sir Henry Smith (the general of the District) in full uniform, with a star and half-a-dozen-medals on his breast." The star of the occasion was notable only by his extreme ordinariness. "Mr. Brown himself, the hero of the day, was the plainest, and simplest man of all; an exceedingly unpretending old gentleman in black, small, withered, white haired, pale, quiet, and respectable." He was as surprised by Brown's willingness to take the limelight as by Lord Stanley's unprepossessing appearance. "I rather wondered why he chose to be the centre of all this

Photograph by "Mr. Keith" or "Mr. Berry," 1857. One of several group photographs of dignitaries celebrating laying of the foundation stone of the Liverpool Free Public Library. Near the end of Hawthorne's term as consul. Courtesy of the Liverpool Record Office.

ceremony, for he did not seem either particularly to enjoy it, or to be at all incommoded by it, as a more nervous and susceptible man might." It is easy to identify all three men on the photograph, particularly the incongruously small and unimpressive central figure.

After describing the locale of the ceremony, Hawthorne wrote, "Two or three photographs were now taken of the site, the cornerstone, Mr. Brown, the distinguished guests, and the crowd at large; then ensued (or followed, I forget which) a prayer from the Bishop of Chester, and speeches from Mr. Holmes, Mr. Brown, Lord Stanley, Sir John Packington, Sir Henry Smith, and as many others as there was time for." Hawthorne

was not at all put out by not having to speak, noting with amusement that Sir Henry Smith had "thrust himself prominently forward, with a view to being called for by the crowd, and then said some pre-considered nothings with a martial force of utterance." He sympathized more with Lord Stanley, who "acquitted himself very creditably, though brought out unexpectedly (at that time) and with evident reluctance."

Hawthorne acquitted himself even more creditably at the banquet which followed: in his role as American Consul, he addressed an audience of over 900, receiving great acclaim. "I got up and proceeded to deliver myself with as much composure as I ever felt at my own fireside," he reported in his notebook, adding with uncharacteristic immodesty, "my speech was about the best of the occasion; and certainly it was better cheered than any other, especially one passage, where I made a colossus of poor little Mr. Brown, at which the audience grew so tumultuous in their applause, that they drowned my figure of speech before it was half out of my mouth." Newspapers concurred, quoting long passages from Hawthorne's speech about relations between America and England and recording the audience's cheers, but Hawthorne confessed to Ticknor on 24 April that he admired his own "pluck in speaking at all," then commented, "I rather wonder at my coming off so well."[2]

The photograph of the foundation stone ceremony preceded Hawthorne's triumph, but it shows him looking completely at ease. He stands at the corner, dressed like everyone but Sir Henry and the Bishop in a topcoat and top hat, and looking straight ahead. After nearly four years of public service, he seems not at all discomfited by public exposure.

Notes

1. On rare occasions, however, a journal could undertake the expense of including a tipped-in image or a pre-printed early form of photogravure.

2. For accounts of the occasion and Hawthorne's speech at the Civic Banquet, see C. E. Frazer Clark, Jr., "An Exhibition Commemorating Nathaniel Hawthorne in England, Liverpool, England, 15–20 July 1971," *Nathaniel Hawthorne Journal* 1972, pp. 203–18 (photograph on p. 213 and news engraving on p. 214); Randall Stewart, "Hawthorne's Speeches at Civic Banquets," *American Literature,* 7 (January 1936): 415–23; and Peter Cowell, *Liverpool Public Libraries: A History of Fifty Years* (Liverpool, 1903). I am grateful to Janet Smith of the Liverpool Record Office for sending a copy of the photograph and information about newspaper coverage.

Photograph for Herbert Fry (1857?)

On 14 December 1856, Hawthorne wrote from Liverpool to Herbert Fry in London, "I am flattered by your wish to obtain a photographic portrait of myself, and shall willingly sit, whenever an opportunity may offer." He expected to be in London the following spring and said, "It will give me great pleasure to promote your views, so far as may be in my power, in reference to the portraits of distinguished Americans." Ten months later, however, he apologized, "I have not had time, since I last wrote you, to pay a visit to London"; but "I shall continue in England some time longer ... and I still hope to fulfill all my engagement with regard to the photograph." With a measure of vanity admixed with regret, he concluded, "It would have been for my interest to sit sooner; for every day seems to have added a grey hair or two to my head, and a deeper line to my face."

On 12 November 1857, Hawthorne sent Fry a brief note addressed from 24 Great Russell Street, Bedford Square, announcing his arrival in London and offering to "be at your commands almost any day that you may appoint," but his awareness that photographs required sunlight made him comment, "I fear that this foggy atmosphere will not be very good for photographic purposes." Five days later, Hawthorne wrote again, presuming his letter had miscarried and repeating that he was in London and available for a sitting: "I should be happy to wait on you for the purpose of being photographed, at any time you might appoint." Apparently Hawthorne was not only willing to sit but eager to do so.

I have not been able to ascertain whether that sitting took place, but an entry in the *British Museum Catalogue of Printed Books* sheds some light on Fry's identity and his project. Under the name of Herbert Fry, listed at 8 York Place on City Road in London, is the entry *"National Gallery of Photographic Portraits,"* sixteen folio issues published in London in 1858. Unfortunately, the copies in the British Museum collection were destroyed by bombings during World War II, and I have not located another set. However, *Humphrey's Journal* for 15 May 1856 announced receiving "a prospectus of a work to be published" that may describe the *National Gallery*: a moderately priced series of excellent "photographic portraits of living celebrities" taken by the famous firm of Maull and Polyblank, to be accompanied by "appropriate biographical no-

Marble bust by Louisa Lander, 1858. Modeled in Rome. Courtesy of the Concord Free Public Library.

Notes

1. *Humphrey's Journal*, 8 (15 May 1856): 32. I am indebted to David Wooters, archivist at the George Eastman House, for assistance with this citation.

Marble Bust by Louisa Lander (1858)

On display at the Concord Free Public Library is a marble portrait bust of Hawthorne, slightly larger than life, made from a clay model completed by Louisa Lander in Rome in April 1858, and presented to the library by the Hawthorne children. George Parsons Lathrop in his "Biographical Sketch" describes the portrait with unqualified admiration, concentrating on the atypical pose:

It is of life-size, and presents the head in a position which raises the chin and inclines the plane of the face slightly backward, so that the effigy might be taken for that of an orator addressing a great audience. This pose was selected by the sculptress because, after due study, she was persuaded that when Hawthorne became interested in conversation and kindled with the desire to set forth his own view, he always raised his head and spoke from a commanding attitude. She chose to perpetuate a momentary action, instead of rendering his customary aspect of holding the chin somewhat down or on a firm level; and this may account for the likeness not being satisfactory to the members of the Hawthorne's own family. The bust, however, renders impressively the magnificent proportions of the neck and head and the whole physiognomy. The mouth is not concealed, and, although it exhibits more decision than that of the Thompson picture, it conveys the same general impression of a quickly responsive sensibility. (pp. 559–60)

The bust was begun at Lander's request on 15 February 1858, soon after the Hawthornes arrived in Rome and visited her studio.[1] Hawthorne felt honored by her request and dutifully spent hours sitting for her. Thus from the beginning of his stay in Italy, Hawthorne was involved with a member of the Roman colony of expatriate artists in a combination of roles: as subject as well as spectator of art, and as a patron as well as

tices, written by Herbert Fry, Esq."[1] Evidently, Fry was a writer and entrepreneur who invited Hawthorne to have his photograph taken for this or a similar publication. What Hawthorne's letters to Fry suggest is that he had been relatively satisfied by his aspect in the Delamotte photograph and the Liverpool photograph, and—more important—that he liked the idea of being included in Fry's projected compendium of "portraits of distinguished Americans."

friend of the artist. Visits were exchanged; Lander dined with the Hawthornes, and she went sight-seeing with them. Further, there was a particular reciprocity in the relationship. As Lander composed Hawthorne's physical portrait, he composed her moral portrait in his notebook, later drawing on it for Hilda, heroine of *The Marble Faun.*

Louisa Lander (1826–1923) was thirty-two when Hawthorne met her and, like himself, a native of Salem. She had come to Rome three years earlier to study under Thomas Crawford and was already noted for her portrait busts (many of statesmen and writers) and for ideal statues (particularly "Virginia Dare"). Her prices were in line with most of the American sculptors, from $20 for plaster to $1,000 for marble, but usually between $100 and $500.[2] When Hawthorne first entered her studio, she seemed an embodiment of youthful enterprise. He reported his impressions in his notebook right after his first sitting:

Miss Lander is from my own native town, and appears to have genuine talent, and spirit and independence enough to give it fair play. She is living here quite alone, in delightful freedom, and has sculptured two or three things that may probably make her favorably known. "Virginia Dare" is certainly very beautiful. During the sitting, I talked a good deal with Miss Lander, being a little inclined to take a similar freedom with her moral likeness to that which she was taking with my physical one. There are very available points about her and her position; a young woman, living in almost perfect independence, thousands of miles from her New England home, going fearlessly about these mysterious streets, by night as well as by day, with no household ties, nor rule or law but that within her; yet acting with quietness and simplicity, and keeping, after all, within a homely line of right. (FIN, pp. 77–78)

Eight months later, when her behavior had allegedly deviated from the "homely line of right," Hawthorne might have lost confidence in his own skill as a character analyst. But during their early acquaintance he was an admirer and a wholly complaisant sitter. Returning from her studio after their first session, he reported, "She asked me not to look at the bust at the close of

the sitting, and, of course, I obeyed; though I have a vague idea of a heavy-browed physiognomy, something like what I have seen in the glass, but looking strangely in that guise of clay" (*FIN,* p. 78).

At the end of March, after a dozen sittings, Lander declared "the clay-model finished" (*FIN,* p. 589). She made final touches the following week, after which Hawthorne gave her partial payment and brought the bust home. He exuberantly reported its reception in a letter to Ticknor on 14 April: "Even Mrs. Hawthorne is delighted with it, and, as a work of art, it has received the highest praise from all the sculptors here, including Gibson, the English sculptor, who stands at the head of the profession." Adding that the Swedish novelist Frederika Bremer "declares it to be the finest modelled bust she ever saw," he urged Ticknor and Fields to try to arrange commissions for Lander on her imminent visit to America. He concluded the letter with his personal judgment: "She is a very nice person, and I like her exceedingly."

Despite the unanimity of opinion on the clay bust that Hawthorne reported, not everyone liked it. Hawthorne's sister Elizabeth saw the photograph of it that Lander brought to Salem and thought "it looked grand, but very old," although as she wrote to Una, Lander promised that the finished "bust will not look old."[3] Julian granted somewhat grudgingly only that it "was a tolerable likeness in the clay."[4]

What became of the clay bust is a mystery, however, and another is what went wrong when it was executed in marble. Despite Lathrop's praise, the marble bust is not a compelling likeness. Julian offered an explanation which at least sounds logical:

A gentleman—I will not mention his name, but he was an American and a person of culture—happened to be in Rome at the time the marble work was proceeding (of course under the hands of the regular workmen employed by sculptors for that purpose, and whose only business it is to reproduce accurately the model placed before them). Hawthorne and Miss Lander were both absent from Rome; and this critic, visiting the studio, noticed what he thought were some errors in the modelling of the lower part of the face, and directed the marble-cutters to make certain altera-

tion, for which he accepted the responsibility. The result was, as might have been expected, that the likeness was destroyed; and the bust, in its present state, looks like a combination of Daniel Webster and George Washington,—as any one may see who pays a visit to the Concord Library, of which institution it is an appurtenance.[5]

The marble bust was completed by the fall of 1858, when Lander had returned to Rome from America and Hawthorne from Florence. But whatever had befallen the marble, worse had befallen the artist. Scandalous accusations were circulating about her, and although a committee of artists urged her to swear her innocence before the American minister, "her pride would not permit this. The wagging tongues of Rome would give her no peace, and there is no doubt that a judgment was generally passed against her...."[6] These events were undoubtedly in Hawthorne's mind when he reported in his pocket diary for 17 October that Cephas Thompson called "& spoke of Miss Lander. What a pity!" Diary entries over the course of the next six weeks report calls by Lander when she was not admitted and notes from her that received only coldly impersonal replies. Clearly the Hawthornes had accepted the art colony's judgment (*FIN*, pp. 615–23).

Lander's personal problems were intermixed with financial difficulties. She had not been offered the public commission she had hoped to obtain in Salem; and in February 1859, the American sculptor John Rogers told friends back home of her troubles in Rome.

I don't think she has sold anything yet but her little Virginia Dare—She has made a figure of Evangeline and put it in marble which is not sold—a bust of Hawthorne which is very good but he does not notice her now and I don't know whether he will take it or not.[7]

Hawthorne did pay for it and he did take it, but only through an intermediary and with none of the delight he had felt in the clay model. After his initial payment of twenty *scudi* after the clay model was completed, he had set aside a hundred "to pay for the bust as the work progresses"—presumably while he was in Florence (*FIN*, pp. 591, 596). Evidently the sum was not

enough. Although he did not communicate with Lander directly, he wrote from England on 11 February 1860, asking Fields, who was then in Rome, to find out how much he still owed her, discreetly indicating his personal disaffection: "For reasons unnecessary to mention, I cannot personally communicate with the lady herself; but I should greatly regret to remain in her debt. The amount being ascertained, will you do me the further favour to pay it...." His judgment of the marble was scathingly direct, though second hand: "The bust, my friends tell me, is not worth sixpence," he wrote. Nonetheless, perhaps recalling the hour-long sittings of the previous year, Hawthorne expressed a modicum of generosity: "but she did her best with it."

The bust had remained with Louisa Lander for display, along with the "Evangeline," first at the Williams' and Everetts' Gallery in Boston and then at the Dusseldorf Gallery in New York in 1860, but a bill of lading indicates that Hawthorne had assumed financial responsibility for its transportation from Italy.[8] There is no way of knowing if Hawthorne ever learned that the bust was acclaimed in both Boston and New York. Presumably the Hawthornes took possession of it after their return to America, whether or not they displayed it, and we may never know the motives that lay behind the children's gift of it to the Concord Library. As for Lander herself, she never did achieve eminence as a sculptor. She returned from Rome to work in relative obscurity in Washington, D.C., until her death.

On one level, Hawthorne was well prepared for disappointment with his finished marble bust. In artists' studios he had seen sketches for paintings that were more vital than the finished canvasses, and clay models whose fine discriminations were lost in the marble. Further, he had often observed that copyists rarely captured the spirit of the artwork they try to replicate (a point he reiterated in *The Marble Faun*), and in a sense the marble was only a copy of the clay. Artists assured him there was "no risk of mischief," but he doubted whether workmen could "repeat" a model accurately (*FIN*, p. 130). Perhaps he recalled Sophia's drawing of Ilbrahim which the engraver had mangled or the disappointing cast of her clay medallion of Charles Emerson. But preparation did not mitigate disappointment.

In large measure his judgments first of the clay

model and then of the marble were merely echoes of other people's opinions. Although he usually deferred to such judgments, it nevertheless seems peculiar that he ventured no observation of his own about the finished bust, especially since he had so carefully cultivated his role as connoisseur throughout his stay in Italy. Perhaps he felt inhibited by his own ambivalence about marble portraiture, expressed in his notebooks and developed in *The Marble Faun*. Kenyon spoke for him when he said that "flitting moments...ought not to be incrusted with the eternal repose of marble" (*MF*, p. 16); but as George Lathrop pointed out, Lander "chose to perpetuate a momentary action," showing Hawthorne with his head raised instead of in his usual posture with "the chin somewhat down or on a firm level." Further, Hawthorne criticized the fashion for portrait busts as an index of egocentricity; he believed that later generations would puzzle over the many mid-century "concretions and pertrifications of a vain self-estimate." Americans' desire for "perpetuating themselves in this mode" amazed him: "And it ought to make us shiver, the idea of leaving our features to be a dusty-white ghost among strangers of another generation" (*MF*, pp. 118–19). Whether or not he shivered, he did leave his marble lineaments to strangers.

According to William Gerdts, Lander might not have been the only sculptor Hawthorne sat for in Rome. Gerdts says Hawthorne was reportedly sculpted by an Italian who was "a kind of heir to Canova working still in the master's former studio. If that is correct, the most likely candidate in Rome would have been Rinaldo Rinaldi."[9] And Moncure D. Conway reported seeing "a bust of Hawthorne now in the possession of his friend and banker, Mr. Hooker, at Rome. It is by Phillips, and is especially interesting as representing the author in early life, before the somewhat severe mouth was modified by a moustache."[10] Of course, there are also posthumous portrait busts, notably the one by Daniel Chester French in the Hall of Fame, unveiled in 1929, and the bust on the portico of the Library of Congress, done by Jonathan Scott Hartley in 1895. Nevertheless, the portrait bust by Louisa Lander is the only one that has come down to us that was made from life.

Aesthetic merit aside, it is unusual in other ways. It was Hawthorne's first sculptured portrait, and indeed the only portrait we have from the period of his association with artists in Italy. He apparently had more sittings for it than for any other portrait; it is the only undraped portrait made in his lifetime, and it is the only one we know he paid for himself. It is also the only one he expected to like but ended up misprizing. Further, it is one of only two professional portraits of him done by women, and the only one of those to come down to us.[11] And finally, it is the only original portrait of Hawthorne on display in Concord.

Notes

1. Hawthorne reached Rome on 20 January, visited Lander 6 February, and began sittings on 15 February, which continued intermittently until early April. For a detailed study, see John L. Idol, Jr., and Sterling Eisiminger, "Hawthorne Sits for a Bust by Maria Louisa Lander, "*Essex Institute Historical Collections*, 114 (October 1978): 207–12. A copy of the bust is in the Essex Institute.

2. For details of Lander's career, see Wayne Craven, *Sculpture in America* (New York: Thomas Y. Crowell, 1968), pp. 178–79 and 332–33, and Frederick A. Sharf, "'A More Bracing Atmosphere': Artistic Life in Salem, 1850–1859," *Essex Institute Historical Collections*, 95 (April 1959): 160–62.

3. Bancroft Library transcript of letter of 12 October 1858 as quoted by James Mellow, *Nathaniel Hawthorne in His Times* (Boston: Houghton Mifflin, 1980), p. 490.

4. *NHW*, II: 183.

5. Ibid.

6. Craven, p. 332.

7. Ibid.

8. The Lemuel Shaw Papers, 1855–1860, Vol. XVI, in the Massachusetts Historical Society, includes a list of the property assigned the owners of four pieces of statuary that arrived in Boston in October 1859, and the Bills of Lading paid by Edward Lander in November. The amounts are $34.98 for Louisa Lander, $28.14 for Harvard College, $14.02 for John Bertram, and $13.15 for Nathaniel Hawthorne, this last presumably for the Lander bust.

9. Letter from William H. Gerdts, 5 July 1979.

10. *Life of Nathaniel Hawthorne* (London: Walter Scott, 1890), p. 199.

11. Another missing portrait is the crayon drawing made of Hawthorne on 21 July 1858 by the English poet Euphrasia Fanny Haworth, a friend of Browning, who had initiated a friendship with Hawthorne in Liverpool shortly after his arrival in 1853. See *FIN*, p. 604.

Sketches by Julian Hawthorne (1859)

The first visual records of the moustache Hawthorne started growing in April 1859 are five sketches by Julian Hawthorne, then thirteen, in an album shared with his mother during the family's residence in Italy.[1] All are busts showing familiar clothing (black jacket, high-collared shirt, and bow tie), and Hawthorne's thick eyebrows and waving hair. But Julian also depicted his father's receding hairline as well as the new moustache, which Sophia thought made him look "like a bandit."

The most detailed of the sketches is a water color, 3 x 2½ inches, in black with flesh tones, showing Hawthorne facing forward and looking meditatively out of the lower right of the twelfth page, hedged by separate drawings of a pencil case, a pen, and a small dish. Clearly, Julian thought well of the sketch: he signed it below and wrote "Nathaniel Hawthorne" above the left shoulder. Among the water colors on the opposite page, in the upper left, is a small pencil sketch which seems to be a preliminary drawing for the first portrait.

On the densely filled twentieth page of the album, Julian made a smaller water color of Hawthorne's right profile, 2½ x 1¾ inches, again in black with flesh tones. A smaller pencil sketch of the right profile is below and to the left. And a pencil sketch, 2 x 1¼ inches, showing Hawthorne's double-chinned left profile, appears three pages later.

Although none of Julian's sketches of his father is a notable work of art, they are all forthright and recognizable. What seems particularly noteworthy is that although Julian presumably caught his father during informal and unguarded momemts, his sketches resemble Hawthorne's formal portraits in pose as well as costume.

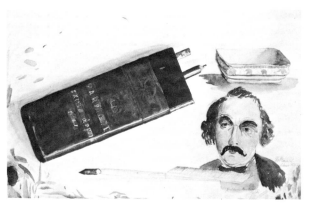

One of five sketches by Julian Hawthorne, 1859. In album shared with his mother. Courtesy of The Bancroft Library.

Notes

1. The black-covered sketchbook, containing drawings by Sophia Hawthorne as well as Julian, ca. 1858 to 1860, is at the Bancroft Library, University of California, Berkeley. Hawthorne noted the date he began growing his moustache in his pocket diary (*FIN*, p. 659), and he reported Sophia's comment in a letter to Ticknor dated 17 June 1859. I am grateful to William Roberts of the Bancroft Library and to Maurice Bassan for their help in acquiring copies of Julian's sketches.

Photographs by J. J. E. Mayall (1860)

At the request of his earliest and closest Liverpool friend, Henry Arthur Bright, Nathaniel Hawthorne was photographed on 19 May 1860 by the renowned portrait photographer, J. J. E. Mayall, in his studio at 224 Regent Street in London. Three portraits were made on that occasion, printed and finished in the "large cabinet size," 6½ x 9 inches. One (later confusingly called the "Motley" photograph) was chosen by Bright. Another (later known as the "Holden" Mayall) was mailed to the London residence of Hawthorne's American friend, the historian John Lothrop Motley, where Hawthorne was a house guest. A third was selected in Mayall's studio and in Hawthorne's presence by Francis Bennoch, Hawthorne's closest London friend and his host after he left the Motleys.[1]

All the original Mayall cabinet poses were three-quarter length, showing Hawthorne seated in a round-backed armchair, his receding hair parted on the left and combed back but full at the sides, and his moustache full, drooping at the ends. He is wearing his usual outfit—a black broadcloth suit, a waist-coat with a ribbed weave, a high-collared white shirt, and a bow-tied black stock. In Bright's "Motley" pose, the chair and body are turned slightly right, Hawthorne's left foot is crossed over his right, his left arm rests loosely at his side, and his right arm is bent. In his right hand he holds a small book with a finger loosely inserted; he is looking to his left with a pleasantly alert expression, and his eyes are wide open. In the "Holden" pose, the chair and body are turned slightly left, pulled up to a table; the right leg is crossed over the left, the right arm rests loosely on the chair, and the left arm is bent, with a finger loosely inserted in a small book set on top of a large book on the table. Hawthorne's face is turned to the right, and his chin and eyes are slightly lowered. In the Bennoch pose, the chair and figure are turned even further left and pulled up to the same table that appeared in the "Holden," but without the small book. Hawthorne's right arm rests loosely beside him on the chair, and his bent left arm is outstretched on the large book. His head is turned slightly left, and the moustache protruding from the side looks particularly droopy; but the eyes look intently forward.

When Hawthorne walked into Mayall's studio with Henry Bright on 19 May, it was three days after his arrival in London for a two-week bachelor fling of social engagements and outings. The letter Bright wrote him the night before clearly indicates that Hawthorne had already agreed to the Mayall sitting, perhaps the previous evening and in John Motley's presence:

If to-morrow is sunshiny enough to photograph you, and if you are not otherwise engaged, well, let us get it done! I shall be here (Oxford and Cambridge Club) at twelve, and again at four, if you will look in at either time.... I was very glad indeed to see Mr. Motley last night.[2]

Bright recalled the occasion over twenty years later, after a controversy had developed about the sitting and the photographs, but his letter to Julian intimates that Mayall took only two poses:

*I went with Hawthorne to the photographer (Mayal) [sic], as he had promised me a photograph of himself. He gave his name, and Mayal came up in a great state of excitement. Hawthorne got very shy, and grasped his umbrella as if it were the last friend left him. This, of course, was taken away from him by the photographer, and a table with a book on it was put in its place. "Now, sir," said Mayal, "please to look **intense!**" He was afterwards told to look smiling (at the portrait of a lady!). I chose the 'intense' one, and afterwards had a copy taken of it for a friend of Hawthorne.... Mayal insisted on my going behind a screen, where your father could not see me. After your father's death the photograph was engraved, and I sent other copies to your mother, Mr. Longfellow, and one or two more. The original (there was only one taken at the time) hangs in my own room.*[3]

After Bright's death, his widow checked his diary record of the sitting and discovered he had first mentioned two poses but corrected the number to three.[4] Possibly his memory made a similar slip when he wrote to Julian over two decades later. His corrected diary notation of three separate poses is substantiated by the pictures themselves and by other reliable testimony. Bennoch himself later reported that Hawthorne took him to Mayall's where he selected a pose distinctly different from Bright's, and Mayall's records establish that a copy of the "Holden" pose was sent to Motley.

At the time Hawthorne sat for him, John Jabez Edwin Mayall (1810–1901) was recognized as one of England's leading photographers. Within a year after arriving in London from Philadelphia in 1846, already a skilled daguerreotypist, he was running the "American Daguerreotype Institution" on the West Strand and winning fame for the clarity and high polish of his large portrait daguerreotypes. In 1852, he moved to a larger establishment at 224 Regent Street, where he began using the newly developed wet plate photographic process, making collodion-coated glass negatives from which he could readily make multiple prints. At the time of Hawthorne's visit in May 1860, Mayall had already begun to take his celebrated photographs of

Queen Victoria and her family, and, in August, fourteen of these were published in carte de visite size as *The Royal Album*. Thousands of copies were sold at once, spreading Mayall's fame and establishing the fashion for photograph albums. Clearly, Bright chose well when he chose Mayall.

When Hawthorne entered Mayall's studio, he sat for a relatively large portrait that was not intended for mass production. Possibly Mayall put two exposures on each of two different glass plates (which would explain why Bright thought at first that only two poses were taken), and soon afterward prints were made of three and possibly all four of them. Then, after Hawthorne's death in 1864, the Mayall studio issued copies of at least two of the poses, most of them as cartes de visite.

A carte de visite photograph is a small albumen print measuring about 2¼ x 3½ inches and mounted on a slightly larger card. With mutli-lens cameras, a photographer could generally take up to eight poses on a single plate, and he could easily copy extant photographs in carte size. Cartes were relatively inexpensive: Mayall charged a guinea a dozen, but since he printed over half a million a year, they were a major source of income. The fashion for distributing and collecting them had erupted at the end of the 1850s, provoking satirical comments and cartoons in newspapers and magazines in England and America; but after the publication of Mayall's *Royal Album*, photograph albums became standard items in Victorian drawing rooms to display carte pictures of friends, family, and celebrities. Queen Victoria collected thirty-six "royal" carte albums of her own. To meet public demand, many photographers badgered public figures for sittings, and it became routine to copy and market pictures of celebrities originally taken by other photographers. An album in the collection of the Massachusetts Historical Society, for example, includes a carte copy of the Mayall "Motley" pose issued by Warren's Studios in Boston. After his return to America, Hawthorne became a cooperative if not enthusiastic participant in the international "cartomania," responding to requests for cartes by sitting for Boston photographers and for the Brady studio in Washington.[5]

It was apparently in the same cooperative spirit that Hawthorne acceded to Bright's request that he be photographed, though as a friend rather than a public figure. Then, after he accompanied Bennoch to Mayall's studio for Bennoch to select a photograph, the whole episode seems to have slipped from his mind. Possibly the photograph Mayall sent to Motley's address was intended for Hawthorne, but there is no evidence that Hawthorne ever ordered any or even acknowledged that any had been taken.

In fact, there is testimony that he denied it. Five weeks after the Mayall sittings, Hawthorne and his family sailed for America from Liverpool, and, according to the letter from Elizabeth Peabody published in the *Salem Gazette* on 31 August 1886, Hawthorne actually said no such photographs were taken.

To begin at the beginning, I will say that very soon after Mrs. Hawthorne's return from Europe in 1860, she told me that Una, on board the steamer coming home, said that when she was at Mr. Bright's in Liverpool just before sailing, she saw a photograph of her father that was ever so much better than any other. The description which Una gave of the photograph was a description of the Lothrop Motley photograph now in the possession of Mrs. Rose Hawthorne Lathrop. Sophia told me that Hawthorne, who heard Una describe it, declared that he had never sat for such a photograph; and when she persisted and afterward reasserted it, the matter became very painful to him, for he thought it one of the illusions of the delirium of her Roman fever. But after his death, when Mr. Bright wrote to Mrs. Hawthorne begging to know if he could do her any service, she wrote to him telling what Una had persisted in declaring, and that she would like to have that photograph. He then sent it; and one day after it came, and Sophia had hung it up in the library, and I went to the Wayside to see her, she took me into the library, without saying a word. I saw it and exclaimed, "I never saw so wonderful a likeness—he seems to be alive!" She said, "Yes. This is the photograph Una saw at Mr. Bright's, and which I asked him to send me, if it really existed. And when I opened the box that contained it, it nearly knocked me backwards, it looked so alive."

By the time Elizabeth Peabody wrote her letter, both

Bright and Sophia were dead, but a Liverpool resident who had long admired Hawthorne, Robert C. Hall, was attempting to "set the record straight" about the Mayall sittings.[6] He visited Bright's widow, saw her husband's photograph of Hawthorne, learned of Bright's corrected diary entry, and found out about Sophia's letters to him.

Sophia had indeed written to Bright on 21 August 1864, three months after her husband's death, requesting a copy of the photograph Una had described. "Una says your photograph of him, the large one, is the finest likeness there is of him," she said. On the same day, Sophia informed Fields of her appeal; then on 3 October, she reported Bright's reply: "It will be a real pleasure to me to get the photograph copied for you, and I will forward it as soon as it is done." Her copy arrived the following month.

Why Hawthorne should have denied that he "sat for such a photograph" is puzzling at best. A story Elizabeth attributed to Motley provides one explanation, though it runs counter to all other evidence: Hawthorne had no idea that his picture was being taken. It seems more likely that Hawthorne's anxiety about Una's health at this time had made him somehow misconstrue what she said, and then deny his own misconstruction. It is also possible that all memory of the Mayall episode almost immediately slipped out of his mind. It is even possible that Elizabeth misunderstood Sophia's original statements.

The question of what photograph Una saw at Bright's house is far easier to answer. She saw the same photograph that Bright copied for Sophia four years later—the photograph sometimes known by Bright's name but more frequently known as the "Motley" pose. Certainly, Sophia's copy was of this pose, showing Hawthorne looking alertly to his left, and Hall saw the original photograph when he visited the Brights.

A minor discrepancy remains about which pose Bright had ordered from Mayall. As Bright told Julian, Mayall had instructed Hawthorne to look intense for one exposure and to smile for another; then Bright said he "chose the intense one." None of the poses shows Hawthorne smiling, but the Bright-"Motley" comes closest to a smile. Possibly in writing to Julian over twenty years after the sitting, Bright forgot which pose he had ordered, though possibly Mayall misunderstood the original order.

The "Bright-Motley" Pose

In November 1864, immediately after receiving her copy of the photograph Bright owned, Sophia wrote to tell him of "the great joy of looking upon such a portrait" and her feeling that she could not thank him "sufficiently for this beautiful noble picture." Immediately she put it on display in the library of the Wayside. Elizabeth reported her own startled response to the "wonderful" likeness, and Fields had a similar reaction.

Fields then wrote to Bright asking for his own copy of the "wonderful photo," because Sophia "cannot part with it even for a few days." He hoped to have an engraving of it prepared "for a new edition of Hawthorne's books." As Bright's daughter told Hall, her father sent a copy to Fields, then others to Hawthorne admirers in both England and America, and she assumed that Mayall had made all those prints from her father's original in September or October 1864, shortly before he retired.

The photograph Bright sent to Sophia Hawthorne later passed on to her daughter, Rose Hawthorne Lathrop. In his comment on the Mayall controversy in the *New York World,* 26 June 1886, Julian Hawthorne described the photograph as one familiar to him "since his youth, and which he last saw a week ago"—presumably at the Lathrops' home. Rose owned at least two copies of the pose, each in the cabinet size of 4 x 5½ inches, both preserved in her album of photographs and family memorabilia now in the Berg Collection.

Rose's albumen print of the entire three-quarter pose is pasted into the center of page 9 of her album, above the pasted signature "Nath' Hawthorne." On a slip of paper beneath, "April 16th" is written next to the printed word "Concord," and the number 2 is written in next to the printed "186," suggesting that the photograph came from an official document Hawthorne submitted at that date. However, given Hawthorne's denial of the Mayall sitting, Sophia's correspondence with Bright, and also the fact that the cabinet photograph was not in general use until the mid-1860s, it

Photograph by J. J. E. Mayall, 1860: the "Bright-Motley" pose. Cabinet copy by Conly. Courtesy of C. E. Frazer Clark, Jr.

Carte issued by Mayall. Courtesy of C. E. Frazer Clark, Jr.

seems likely that Rose acquired the photograph well after 1862. Possibly this photograph is the one Sophia received from Bright in the fall of 1864. Given Bright's generosity and his affection for Hawthorne, however, he might have ordered Sophia's copy in the double size of his own photograph.

The second cabinet-sized albumen print of the "Bright-Motley" pose in Rose's album, showing the figure cut off below the first waistcoat button, is pasted into the upper center of page 6. Underneath it, Rose copied her own description of her father's appearance, appropriate to this relatively smiling pose:

His face was sunny. There was the perpetual gleam of a glad smile on his mouth and in his eyes.... His large eyes, liquid with light, and deep with dark shadows, told me even when I was very young that he was in some respects different from other people. I was fully aware he could see through me as if I were a soul in one of his own books.

Rose obviously admired this photograph and felt that this was one of the best ever made of her father, as she told the art collector and critic Charles Henry Hart in a letter of 14 October 1897. She commented that "a large lithographic portrait [from it] prepared by the publishers Houghton, Mifflin & Co., for use in schools" was one of the best known.[7]

The lithograph to which she referred had been copyrighted in 1883 and was then widely distributed. An 1884 newspaper clipping in Robert Hall's scrapbook announces the addition of this life-sized print to Houghton Mifflin's collection of authors' portraits, quoting Rose's approval of its pleasant alertness:

It is enlarged from an English photograph and represents the author as he appeared in the vigor and the grace of his happiest and strongest days. His daughter, Mrs. Lathrop says: "It is this aspect which, when it recurred later in life, always seemed to me to be his most individual expression."

The lithograph, printed by the Armstrong Company, is signed in the stone "J. E. Baker," presumably the signature of the Boston-born Joseph E. Baker, a fellow-apprentice of Winslow Homer. Many prints have survived, some with the addition of chalk highlights that convey the impression that they are "originals." The Library of Congress owns one print, a framed copy hangs in the lobby of the Hawthorne Inn, and another is stored at the Essex Institute.

Although the lithograph was probably the best-known version of the "Bright-Motley" pose at the end of the century, copies of the photograph were commercially distributed by the Mayall firm from at least 1867, the date Hall reported acquiring his own print. On the inside cover of his scrapbook, Hall pasted his son's copy of his Mayall print of the half-figure, noting that it was the same as the etching in the second volume of Julian's biography, and "both the same as the Bright Photo to only the latter is nearly full figure; and which is really what the Americans call 'the Motley photo!'"

Several American firms produced their own copies. A cabinet print issued by the Boston photographer Conly was acquired by George H. Holden, a Salem-born Hawthorne admirer, who sent a copy to Mayall's son, who in turn sent it to Hall, complaining about its excessive retouching. Another copy, retained by Holden, is now owned by Frazer Clark. Prints issued by Warren's Studio in Boston are in the collections of the National Archives and the Massachusetts Historical Society, as well as the Essex Institute, and the Essex Institute copy was reproduced in the Salem *Proceedings* and in later volumes including Edward Wagenknecht's *Nathaniel Hawthorne: Man and Writer.*[8] Lathrop was not exaggerating when he said that "the head, with the half-figure, has been reproduced by various photographers, who have sold great numbers of impressions."

Lathrop was of course familiar with the prints of this pose that his wife Rose had owned for years, and her enthusiasm might have colored the description in his "Biographical Sketch," written before he knew any other Mayall photographs existed. The image of Hawthorne, sitting with a book on his knee, his finger marking his place, and "a dawning smile, a bright expectant glance" on his face seemed to reveal his essential character:

The resulting portraiture showed him absolutely as he was: a breathing form of human nobility; a strong, masculine, self-contained nature, stored in a stalwart frame— the face grown somewhat more rotund than formerly, through material and professional success, and lighted up with captivating but calm geniality; while over the whole presence reigned an exquisite temperance of reserve, that held every faculty in readiness to receive and record each finest fluctuation of joy or sorrow, of earnest or of sport.

Lathrop concluded his description and his entire section on Hawthorne's portraits by commenting, "Such as he there appears, we shall do well to imagine him to ourselves."[9]

Julian Hawthorne owned his own card copy of the "Bright-Motley," the model for the etching to which Hall referred. In his 1886 *World* article on Hawthorne's portraits, Julian took pains to establish that the etching in his biography was not based on his sister's photograph but on one he had acquired for himself, "a copy of the head alone, carte de visite size, which was published in London, purchased there in 1874, and which bore on its back the legend, 'Mayall, London.'" A few months later, in a letter of 16 September to Holden, rejecting the thesis that Mayall had made only one photographic portrait of Hawthorne—the one recently engraved for *Harper's* and eventually known by Holden's name—Julian said that his carte was unquestionably a copy of a Mayall original:

Etching by Stephen Alonzo Schoff, 1884. Prepared for *Nathaniel Hawthorne and His Wife*, from Julian Hawthorne's Mayall carte.

Wood engraving, 1865. Commissioned by James T. Fields for *Good Company for Every Day in the Year*.

I bought this carte in London some ten or twelve years ago: it was dim, but of the same size as the original. I colored it with water-colors, in order to preserve it, and it was from this that Schoff made his excellent etching. It had Mayalls stamp on it; and I do not think the laws of English copyt. would admit of its having been taken from a photograph by another photographer.[10]

The etching of his carte-sized bust in *Nathaniel Hawthorne and His Wife* is one of the three portraits of Hawthorne which he includes, all prepared by Stephen Alonzo Schoff (see pp. 22 and 96). Schoff's lively and elegant etching of the "Bright-Motley" bust was also printed separately, bearing the monogram "SAS" on the left, and "Etched by S. A. Schoff" imprinted at the bottom. Separate prints were struck, and a few are still on the market. A slightly more elaborated print with a circular decorative border was published in the *Outlook* in 1901. A delicate bust etching reminiscent of Schoff's was made by the award-winning artist William Baxter Palmer Closson (1848–1926) and published in a small portfolio of original etchings entitled *Homes and Haunts of the Poets*.[11]

Although the "Bright-Motley" image is chiefly known today through the Schoff etching commissioned for Julian's biography and the Baker lithograph Rose praised, there are many other graphics based on the pose, including three relatively early ones. The first has unusual interest—an unsigned engraving commissioned by Fields from Sophia's photograph in December 1865 and published almost immediately in *Good Company for Every Day in the Year,* illustrating an excerpt from *The Dolliver Romance* entitled "Little Pansie."[12] Commenting on the two proofs of the engraving she received from Fields in December, Sophia complained that the mouth was awry and that the engraver had completely missed the delicacy and grace of the original photograph. The children disagreed: Julian liked it, Rose did not, and Una was in between. But Sophia begged Fields to see if the engraving might be altered to look less "clumsy and earthly." Then after encountering the published engraving three months later, she told Fields she "felt

Wood engraving, 1872. In *Harper's New Monthly Magazine*.

faint and wan to meet such an earthly, soulless face with the name of Hawthorne attached to it" and begged him not to use it again. "No likeness is much better than an untrue one," she insisted. It is true that the eyes stare more than in the photograph, and the bottom lip is slightly lowered on the right; but Sophia's complaint seems excessive. To the ordinary eye, the engraving is simply another variant of the "Bright-Motley" image.

Five years later, a second unsigned bust engraving of the "Bright-Motley" with the image reversed first appeared in McCabe's *Great Fortunes and How They Were Made,* with a dour and fat-cheeked visage appropriate to a descendant of Puritans and sea captains but barely recognizable as Hawthorne.[13]

Another unsigned wood engraving was published in *Harper's New Monthly Magazine* in October 1872, accompanying Richard H. Stoddard's unsigned biographical commentary on Hawthorne. Sophia would have found this heavy-faced, thick-necked, bull-chested portrait intolerable; but it was the first of the Mayall images to appear in a periodical. Harper's liked the image

well enough to repeat it in 1875 and to issue it as a separate print.

Two undated bust engravings of about the same period are at the National Portrait Gallery. The one issued by J. O. Wright is signed in the plate and on the print "T. Johnson," the same Thomas Johnson who engraved the "Holden" Mayall as well as the Whipple daguerreotype for the *Century* in 1886. The other, printed by James H. Lamb, was engraved by H. B. Hall and Sons (London-born engraver and etcher Henry Bryan Hall [1808–1884] working with his three sons in his New York studio). The "Bright-Motley" image also appears in a number of late nineteenth-century composite photographs of American authors, such as Notman's "Authors Group" of 1882.

Many "Bright-Motley" variants appeared on the centenary of Hawthorne's birth; for example, the Prints and Photographs Division of the Library of Congress preserves two photographs of clay bas reliefs deposited in 1904, one by Sarah W. Symonds and the other by R. B. Goddard. Recent variants of the "Bright-Motley" include a 1936 engraving by Max Rosenthal at the Massachusetts Historical Society, the signed pencil portrait by Jacques Reich in the Berg Collection of the New York Public Library, and the woodcut Ben Shahn made for the 1956 Vintage Jubilee edition of Hawthorne's short stories. Undistinguished variants may often be encountered in commercial publications, such as insurance company calendars and souvenir pamphlets.

The curious attachment of Motley's name to the photograph that Bright commissioned is part of an elaborate controversy that proliferated through the 1880s. Elizabeth Peabody told George Holden that John Lothrop Motley claimed he had arranged for Hawthorne to be photographed surreptitiously and that only one photograph of him was taken. In a letter to the *Salem Gazette* for 10 March 1885, signed "G. H. H.," Holden summed up the account he thought Hawthorne's family accepted. According to Holden, Motley had schemed with a London photographer to take a picture without Hawthorne's knowledge, and four copies were printed—two for Motley, one for Bright, and one for Bennoch—before the negative was accidentally broken. Thus the photograph Una saw at Bright's house (i.e., the photograph Bright copied for Sophia) was the one

Etching by Thomas Johnson. Reversed version of "Bright-Motley" image. Courtesy of the National Portrait Gallery.

Line engraving by H. B. Hall and Sons. Courtesy of the National Portrait Gallery.

Motley had secretly obtained.

Julian Hawthorne scornfully rejected this account. In a brief letter to the *Salem Gazette* dated 15 April 1885, he insisted that "there is not, and never was, an iota of truth in 'G. H. H.'s' assertions about the photograph of Hawthorne," a point he thought adequately established in his recent biography. He had devoted two pages of *Nathaniel Hawthorne and His Wife* to summarizing the "mythical" account, which Lathrop's "Biographical Sketch" also accepted, and then he refuted it. He began,

J. Lothrop Motley, who well knew Hawthorne's aversion to photographic processes, set a trap for his friend in this wise. He invited him to walk one day in London; and as they were passing the studio of a well-

known photographer, Motley asked Hawthorne to step in and make a selection from some pictures of himself, which were ready, he supposed, for examination. They entered, chatting pleasantly together, Hawthorne at the time being in the best of spirits. Dropping into a chair, which Motley placed for him, he looked brightly after his friend disappearing behind a screen in quest of the proofs. At this moment, and with this look of animation upon his face, the photograph referred to was taken, the artist having made all necessary preparations to capture a likeness from the unsuspecting sitter. Motley's proofs were produced and examined, and Hawthorne was never told that he had been taken. This was shortly before the family returned home. One of the children, it seems—I think it was the ethereal Una,—had seen the surreptitious picture at Motley's or at Bennoch's, and on the homeward voyage she referred to it, and said it was a beautiful likeness, far better than she had ever seen before. Hawthorne, of course, was incredulous, and assured his wife that the child must be mistaken. After her husband's death, Mrs. Hawthorne became acquainted with the facts as above narrated, and at her earnest entreaty the photograph was sent to her.

Julian concluded his narrative with a flat denial:

This story is a real curiosity in fabrication. There is not one syllable of truth in it from beginning to end; but the ingenious and elaborate manner in which it is worked up from point to point is remarkable, showing as it does that the writer was in no respect laboring under a misapprehension, or suffering from a defective memory or incomplete information, but that he was consciously inventing all the way through, and enjoying his invention.[14]

At this point Julian introduced Bright's letter with its entirely different first-hand account, concluding with Bright's unequivocal statement, "The account of the photograph being taken for Mr. Motley is quite wrong."

Julian's attack spurred Holden to action. In a hand-written summary of the entire episode prepared after it was all over, he said he "wrote a letter to the *Salem Gazette* concerning a certain photo of Hawthorne," which Julian considered "'a curiosity in fabrication.'" Holden then said,

I immediately undertook to verify the story & in the course of my investigations succeeded in unearthing a negative, somewhere in England, from a sitting given by Hawthorne to the Elder Mayall
This was engraved for Harpers—it appeared, I think, in the number for June 1886
Still another portrait of Hawthorne, the result of my enquiries, appeared, perhaps a year later, in the Century.

Although Holden misleadingly suggested that he himself had unearthed a Mayall negative in England and

turned up "another portrait of Hawthorne," it is true that he spurred those discoveries. By the time of the *Harper's* issue of July (not June) 1886, he had a new theory. After Mayall's son discovered one of his father's photographs that obviously differed from the "Bright-Motley," Holden became convinced that this was the one and only Mayall photograph. In the "Editor's Easy Chair" of the July *Harper's*, George W. Curtis accepted this hypothesis.

Julian then published a scathing attack on Holden in the *World* on 26 June 1886, contemptuously dismissing him as merely a man who "had the misfortune to be born in Salem and who has devoted considerable time and pains to an investigation of Hawthorne as a man and a writer and a sitter to photographers." Again Julian summarized the Motley "invention" Holden had published the year before, concluding with an ironic attack on Elizabeth Peabody as well as Holden:

Such is the story which, we understand, Mr. Holden claims to have written, and which he obtained from a near relative of Hawthorne, who received it, as she believes, from Motley himself some years later, and Mr. Holden now maintains that the photograph from which the engraving in the current Harper was made is, in fact, the identical photograph which the united cunning of Messrs. Motley and Mayall succeeded in stealing from the unsuspecting Hawthorne.

Julian could not believe that Motley would resort to trickery, that deception was needed to obtain Hawthorne's portrait, or that Hawthorne could have held his gaze at the disappearing Motley long enough for a photograph to be made. Judging from the existence of Bright's picture and the one engraved for *Harper's*, as well as information that Bennoch had recently rediscovered his own missing photograph, Julian sensibly concluded that Mayall had undoubtedly taken three separate poses.

After reading her nephew's article, Elizabeth Peabody addressed a letter to the editor of the *Salem Gazette*, published on 31 August, saying that she felt "bound in conscience and honor to Mr. Holden to answer publicly," because she had told him the story she heard "from Mr. Motley's own lips."

He said, "That photograph I gave to Mr. Bright. I got it without Hawthorne's knowing it, during the week in which he was visiting me in London. I had succeeded in showing him the lions and even in lionizing him somewhat without his being aware of it.... We were walking down Oxford street together one day and I said, 'what a bore it is to sit for a photograph, (to which he heartily assented) but nevertheless I have yielded to Mary's importunity, and have been sitting for mine, and I wish you would go in with me and help me decide which is the least bad.' And he assenting, we went into the photographer's."

To accommodate Bright's statement that he had arranged a Mayall sitting, Elizabeth proposed a new hypothesis: Motley had arranged for the surreptitious "Bright-Motley" photograph to be taken not by Mayall but by another London photographer and Bright later had sent a copy of that photograph to Sophia but mistakenly thought it was "the photograph he had taken so much pains to get" at Mayall's. She then attacked Julian's attack, blaming her nephew for "abnormal impetuosity of temperament, preventing all reflective self-criticism; a fault that has led him into all the mistakes of his literary and practical life," a fault which she believed marred his biography of his parents.

Julian commented on his aunt's statement a few weeks later in a letter refusing Holden's mollifying offer of a copy of Bennoch's photograph. He said that "Mr. Motley was not incapable of of [*sic*] playing a joke, though the lady might be incapable of understanding it." He then offered measured praise: "She endows everyone with her own sincerity." Although Julian's hypothesis that Motley would joke with the sober Elizabeth seems far-fetched, it is easier to accept than the alternatives: that the earnest Elizabeth invented the story, that the trustworthy historian had lied or fantasized about it, or (as Lathrop suggested) that Motley told a white lie that developed into an established "tradition."

But in his effort to resolve the discrepancies in the story of Motley's involvement, Lathrop only translated them into something more baroque. Perhaps Motley had not arranged for a sitting, he suggested in his *Century* article of April 1887, but after hearing that Hawthorne had been photographed by Mayall at Bright's

Photograph by J. J. E. Mayall, 1860: the "Holden" pose. Mayall carte courtesy of C. E. Frazer Clark, Jr.

request, Motley might have gone to Mayall "to secure a copy of that likeness." Lathrop wildly speculated that "Mayall perhaps brought out the plate which he had made surreptitiously, and this pleased Motley.... [He] would of course say to his friends that the photograph had been made without Hawthorne's knowledge; and in this way the tradition, with the facility of transformation belonging to all tradition, would become established, that Motley himself had arranged a little plot for obtaining a photograph of Hawthorne unawares."

Although Lathrop agreed with Julian that Mayall had made three separate photographs, his hypothesis about Motley's acquisition of a surreptitious pose is as fantastic as Elizabeth's hypothesis about Motley's plot. Both assumed that Motley deviously secured the near-smiling pose of Hawthorne which became identified by Motley's name. Hall's rejection of this thesis is evident in the punctuation of his scrapbook notation about that pose: it was "what the Americans call 'the Motley Photo!'" In the Salem *Proceedings* and in later publications, the image is identified as "the so-called Motley photograph." Hall himself called it the "Bright Photo," which seems more accurate. Perhaps the double name of "Bright-Motley" can at least eliminate the misleading associations conveyed by the name of Motley alone.

The "Holden" Pose

The story of how the "Holden" Mayall became known in America is slightly less intricate than the "Bright-Motley" story, but it has its own share of mystery, peculiarity, and even absurdity. The absurdity begins with its identification as the "Holden" photograph, a consequence of the mistaken assumption promoted by Holden himself that the image remained unknown for twenty-six years until he "unearthed" it. But the image had not been buried, at least not at the beginning of its existence.

Clear proof comes from Robert Hall. Next to the carte of the picture in his scrapbook is his notation that he had acquired it in 1865, and he added that an engraving based on the same image had been published in an English edition of *Our Old Home* the preceding year. J. J. E. Mayall, Jr., who also saw that engraving, not only agreed that it was a "poor job" but concluded it was not based on a Mayall print but on another firm's poor copy. Possibly when the senior Mayall prepared copies of the "Bright-Motley" portrait after Hawthorne's death he also issued copies of this other image, but, for whatever reason, it never had wide currency.

The story of how that image resurfaced after an interval of twenty years belongs to a sequence of events that Holden initiated in October 1886 by writing to Mayall's son, who had taken over his father's firm. What Holden was looking for was validation of his story about the "Bright-Motley" photograph and not a new photograph. At this point Mayall, Jr., became the

detective and made a series of related discoveries.

First, after discussing the matter with his father and searching through old records and portfolios, he came up with his father's unfaded copy of the photograph that showed Hawthorne looking meditatively to his right. He also found his father's record that a copy had been sent to John Lothrop Motley at 31 Hertford Street, London, in May 1860—whether it was ordered by him or (as Bright's widow later suggested) intended for his house guest, Nathaniel Hawthorne. Mayall, Jr., subsequently learned what happened to that copy: after Motley's death it went to his daughter, Mrs. Mary Sheridan of Dorsetshire, and she still retained it, though in faded condition. In the meantime, Mayall copied his father's photograph, copied his father's entry onto the back, and sent it off to Holden, thus setting Holden off on a separate line of action.

But Mayall kept on looking for his father's original negative, and eventually he found one, the only one remaining from the 1860 sitting. He generously printed up copies not only for Holden but for Hall, a new participant in the fray. Stimulated by his discovery, Mayall planned to publish it in the form of a photogravure, but, as he wrote Hall on 6 June 1887, his plans ended in total frustration.

He had given the glass plate to an "excellent man" who promised to prepare a photogravure. The man made a plate, but some further work seemed required. Mayall then turned the plate over to an expert engraver, who decamped with it and sold it to another engraver, who then used it for trade catalogues. At the time of his letter to Hall in June 1887, Mayall was trying to stop publication and recover his plate, but with almost no hope of success; and he lamented that even if he did recover it, he might not be brave enough to publish it. "There seems to be a kind of fatality about these photos of Hawthorne," he wrote, and "misfortune and unpleasantness for me."

But the photograph he had sent Holden over a year earlier brought Holden a measure of fame and fortune. Convinced that he was responsible for its discovery and that consequently the photograph was "his," Holden set about retailing it. He believed that this was the photograph Motley had surreptitiously arranged and the only one Mayall took, and, in this double light, he offered it in the summer of 1885 to *Harper's Magazine*, which four years earlier had published his article on "Hawthorne Among His Friends."

Holden's correspondence with the editor of *Harper's Magazine* over a period of seven months displays his tenacious eagerness to exploit an advantage and, at the same time, offers privileged glimpses into some of the practices of one of America's leading magazines. On 7 August 1885, *Harper's* editor H. M. Alden thanked Holden for "his" copy of the Mayall photograph and asked what compensation he wanted for its use as an engraved frontispiece. Clearly, Alden was taken with Holden's contention that it was the only Mayall photograph in existence and that it had been made without Hawthorne's knowledge. He stipulated, "We must, of course have Mr. Mayall's permission to copy the photograph—as our Magazine is published in England." He asked Holden to write up its history but suggested it "would receive more prominence if Mr. George W. Curtis would incorporate it in his 'Easy Chair,' as coming from you—if you have no objection to the appearance of your name in this connection." To sweeten the suggestion, he said "We would also give your name as the owner of the photograph in our title to the portrait."

Holden evidently tried to expand his role by sending Alden copies of other photographs he had obtained. On 16 October, Alden thanked him for a "Boston" photograph as well as the "Bright-Motley" photograph, but said *Harper's* would stick to the original plan of publishing only one image. He again encouraged Holden to write out his account of Motley's trickery, "making as clear as possible the exceptional value of this particular portrait, from the circumstances under which it was taken, & avoiding controversy." The fifty dollar enclosed check he called "simply a recognition of material value, which still leaves us under obligation to you for your kind preference shown us in this matter."

Nearly four months later, on 5 February 1886, Alden sent Holden a proof of Thomas Johnson's engraving of the "Holden" pose, saying "I hope the result will seem to you satisfactory." He also sent a copy to James Russell Lowell, requesting an article. Responding to another offer from Holden—this time of Bennoch's photograph—Alden said he would like to see it, asking

him to "postpone exhibition of the new portrait" to anyone else.

Holden must have sent the "new" Bennoch almost immediately. On 17 February, Alden said it was "the most pleasing portrait of Hawthorne that I have seen" but declined to engrave it because "it has not the absolute novelty which belongs to the engraving we have already made"—that is, the novelty of its supposed origin in Motley's trickery. Lowell had praised the engraving as "by far the most satisfactory likeness of Hawthorne that he has seen," though he could not write about it for *Harper's*, "being already pledged to the *Atlantic* in the matter of Hawthorne." (Lowell never did write about the portrait for either the *Atlantic* or *Harper's*, but Curtis would quote his comment in the "Easy Chair.") Then, the same day that he refused the Bennoch, Alden told Holden in a second letter that because Curtis considered it "the best he has ever seen," he would again "consult the house" about engraving it. On 8 March, however, he simply said, "Let the Century get the other picture if it wants it," adding confidently that even if they took it, *Harper's* would "come out with ours first—probably in the July No." Meanwhile, Holden sent Alden a new account of the photograph, omitting references to Motley's supposed trickery. Alden then questioned why Holden had abandoned that "pretty" story of Motley's subterfuge, which was "the especially novel point in the whole matter." Perhaps it was Holden's correspondence with Mayall and others, together with Julian's angry refutations, that finally persuaded him to relinquish the account. Nevertheless, he still believed that "his" picture was the only one Mayall had ever made.

The engraving of the "Holden" by Thomas Johnson appeared as the frontispiece to *Harper's* in July 1886, identified as "from a photograph by Mayall, London, 1860." It is a well-defined white-line wood engraving presenting a complex and compassionate figure—a good engraving, as Hall had noted, if "not so like as" the original photograph, which captured what Mayall, Jr., called Hawthorne's "real nature." Lathrop offered a more specific criticism in his *Century* article the following year: although Mayall had carefully posed Hawthorne with a "deliberate arrangement of the finger between the book-leaves," this arrangement was "ig-

White-line wood engraving by Thomas Johnson, 1886. In *Harper's*.

Wood engraving by "E. S.," 1894. In *Harper's*.

nored and obliterated by the burin which traced that block." Johnson reproduced only the half-figure, eliminating the hands. *Harper's* would make good use of this portrait, however. Cut off below the first waistcoat button, it appears as the frontispiece to an 1893 Harper's publication, Horatio Bridge's *Personal Recollections of Nathaniel Hawthorne;* and it was issued as one of *Harper's* series of "Black and White Prints."

Johnson's technique in this engraving is as representative of the 1880s as the *Ballou's* and *Boston Museum* wood engravings were typical of the 1850s. By the time Johnson engraved one Mayall photograph and Timothy Cole another, the swift short lines of white-line wood engraving had largely replaced the long sweeping lines of mid-century black-line wood engrav-

ing. Photographs could be printed directly onto the woodblock, and engravers could achieve subtle textural gradients by "drawing with white into the black," as Estelle Jussim puts it, using delicate "dots and flicks to describe *the light falling on objects*." and to distinguish a wide range of blacks, grays, and whites.[15] According to Weitenkampf (p. 132), "Thomas Johnson, who excelled in portraits, won praise for his 'calm and appropriate treatment.'" The fact that we have three of his "calm and appropriate" treatments of Hawthorne suggests how prolific and how popular he must have been.

For whatever reason, *Harper's* commissioned a more abbreviated half-length engraving of the "Holden" to accompany Howells's account of meeting Hawthorne in "My First Visit to New England," published in *Harper's New Monthly Magazine* in 1894. The artist is merely identified as "T. V." and the engraver as "E. S."

Two years earlier, the "Holden" image was used for the bust on the bronze medallion commissioned by the Grolier Club in 1892. "The model has been made with much care by the well-known French sculptor and medallist, Ringel d'Illzach," the Club announced on 14 February 1893, issuing a leaflet with a half-tone reproduction of the seven-inch bas relief medallion offered for sale at ten dollars and specifying that "the metal will be of the finest quality, and will be cast by one of the most skillful founders." D'Illzach's plaster model remains in the possession of the Grolier Club.[16]

Copies of the original "Holden" photograph are rare, but Frazer Clark owns two Mayall bust prints, reproduced in the *Nathaniel Hawthorne Journal* for 1975 and 1977. A cabinet print of the "so-called Holden photograph" made by the Salem photographer Frank Cousins is at the Essex Institute and was published in the Salem *Proceedings*. The cabinet print of the entire three-quarter pose recently acquired by the Huntington Library might be one of those made by Mayall's son from his father's negative: deep space surrounds the figure, and wrinkles on the face and on the clothing are clearly delineated.

In his "Easy Chair" article of July 1886, George Curtis included some rambling comments on "the Hawthorne portraits, of which many have been published," saying of the "Holden," "That which is the frontispiece of this number of the Magazine Mr. Lowell thinks to be the best that he knows." He added, "It is very pleasant to look upon the picture of a face once so familiarly known—the face of a man of genius in his prime—and to think that the quiet, modest author ... is now beheld of all men with gratitude and reverence as one of the benefactors of the world." Next, Curtis gave Holden's new theory of how this photograph was taken—modifying Bright's account by maintaining that only one negative was made by Mayall. The only fresh information in the "Easy Chair" is what Mayall, Jr., had recently told Holden: "'I have a distinct recollection of Mr. Hawthorne—just as he sat for the photo. I remember remarking that he looked very like a Frenchman. My view of him was a momentary glance from the door of the dark room, where at that time I had charge of the chemical processes.'" Mayall, Jr., considered the photograph "remarkably good," a result of the sitter's cooperation during a relatively long exposure time.

*Such a negative, **at that date**, could not be ordinarily produced with a less exposure than thirty or forty seconds in the camera, with the subdued light usually employed in my father's studio. Hawthorne must have remained quite still during these thirty or forty seconds, for the print shows plainly the iris of his eyes, and individual hairs in his eyebrows and mustache.*

Curtis then repeated Mayall's account of finding his father's record of a Hawthorne sitting, his reasons for concluding no negative had survived, then his "diligent search ... for the senior Mayall's own copy, ... finally discovered in an old portfolio"—the copy reproduced for Holden and engraved by Johnson, before Mayall found his father's original negative. Like Holden, Curtis mistakenly assumed that Mayall's discovery of only one image proved that only one existed, and therefore believed that neither the Bennoch nor what he called the "Lothrop Motley" photograph was made by Mayall.

Robert C. Hall of Liverpool entered the scene after reading Curtis's convoluted account. Determined to "set the record straight," he communicated with Mrs. Bright, Bennoch, and Holden, as well as with Mayall, Jr. What he learned from the photographer provides a special perspective on the entire group of photographs and on photographers' practices and aesthetic standards at the time the Mayall photographs were taken.

In a series of letters in October 1886, Mayall, Jr., explained why the story attributed to Motley was utterly unbelievable: it was impossible for his father to take the "Holden" pose surreptitiously or instantaneously. To begin with, the pose was carefully arranged. It was one of his father's favorites—as was the "Bright-Motley"—adopted during the daguerreotype days because it could be held for up to a minute with relative ease. Even after the wet collodion process speeded up exposure times, his father still used those poses; in many photographs in his files, an individual sits with his legs crossed and his finger in a book. And Mayall, Jr., also said that the diffused light and the depth of focus in the Hawthorne photographs clearly indicated that his father had used an exposure of thirty to forty seconds. Although a relatively instantaneous exposure of ten or twelve seconds was possible in 1860 in direct sunlight, this would have resulted in deep shadows.

Photograph by J. J. E. Mayall, 1860: the "Bennoch" pose. Copy by Frank Cousins. Courtesy of the Essex Institute.

He also commented on retouching procedures in his father's day. Here he used as evidence the Conly cabinet copy of the "Bright-Motley," his own print from the negative for his father's "Holden," and Hall's carte copies of both poses. He could easily tell that the Conly had been copied from a photograph that had stippling on the face—what we call "finished in Indian [*sic*] ink," he said, and with "artificial background as we used formerly to make in all our larger prints 'finished in Indian ink.'" Despite his evident distaste for such stippling and background, he concluded that the Conly was probably copied from "one of ours." He preferred Hall's carte copy of that pose because it showed little retouching. But Hall's copy of the "Holden" was "poor"

by contrast with his own print from the glass plate negative which had no retouching at all and was therefore wholly "truthful." On these purist grounds he criticized Thomas Johnson's engraving because it lacked the "real nature" of the original photograph, and Hall readily agreed. Beneath the Johnson engraving pasted into his scrapbook he noted that it was "very good but not so like as the photo' it is copied from, which I have."

Mayall clearly established another point: both the "Bright-Motley" and "Holden" photographs originated in his father's studio, both originally printed there in the same "large Royal cabinet size" of 6½ x 9 inches, which his father favored for portraits. He had nothing to say about the Bennoch photograph, which Hall himself did not get to see until two months later.

The "Bennoch" Pose

What happened to Bennoch's photograph can be told more succinctly than the other two Mayall narratives, but this tale too includes an intricate dramatic episode and a few incidental curiosities. It is the only one of the three stories which involved someone privy to the 1860 sitting in the tangled controversies of the mid-1880s, Hawthorne's old friend Francis Bennoch. Holden began writing to him in August 1885 soon after writing to Mayall, and there is truth to Holden's statement that the Bennoch photograph was engraved for the *Century* in consequence of his inquiries. But in his curious self-magnification, Holden gave no credit to the person directly responsible for providing him with the photograph, Bennoch himself.

In letters to both Holden and Robert Hall, Bennoch recalled the occasion when Hawthorne "gave" him the photograph in May 1860, presumably between 29 and 31 May, when Hawthorne was his guest at Blackheath. "Hawthorne took me to Mayall & there I selected the photo I liked the best," he told Hall. His first letter to Holden had recounted that occasion and also reported his attempt to order a duplicate soon after: Mayall could not locate the negative and assumed it had been accidentally broken. The framed original had a place of honor in Bennoch's library, and "Una, who was a frequent, and welcome, visitor at our house admired it greatly." When Bennoch first saw Bright's photograph near the end of 1886, and observed that they were both in the same large cabinet size, Bennoch concluded his had a more characteristically meditative expression. "At all events I prefer it!" he told Hall.

The most dramatic episode in the history of his photograph was its "loss" over twenty years after it was first taken and its later recovery, a story Bennoch told to both Holden and Hall. A London artist named Fred Piercy, who was making a portrait of Bennoch, asked to borrow the Hawthorne photograph as the basis for a life-sized crayon portrait to include in his collection of famous men of letters. Piercy planned to sell permanently finished photographic copies of his drawing at about a guinea each, and Bennoch gladly agreed to this mode of sharing what he considered the "best likeness ever taken of Hawthorne." Both he and Julian watched its progress. Then, after the drawing was completed and Bennoch requested return of his photograph, Piercy insisted that he had given it to Julian to deliver. By this time Julian had returned to America, and Bennoch sorrowfully assumed that he had simply appropriated his father's photograph. But four or five years later, in November 1885, Holden's inquiries spurred him to raise the issue with Piercy once again at a moment when Piercy's son happened to be present. Young Piercy recalled seeing the photograph in the room behind his father's studio and immediately brought it forth. It was dusty, and Hawthorne's face looked out through shattered glass; but the photograph itself was "happily uninjured."

The photograph had faded, however, and soon after recovering it, Bennoch had it copied by a "scientific artist" who was able to recapture its original freshness. He then ordered half a dozen proofs from the negative before having it retouched. In January 1886, he sent Holden a copy of what he called the "Bennoch-Hawthorne Portrait," the one Holden almost immediately offered to *Harper's* and later to the *Century*. At the same time, Bennoch told Holden he planned to send six "finished pictures" from the retouched negative, five for distribution to Rose Lathrop, Julian Hawthorne, Elizabeth Peabody, his Boston friend Mr. Houghton, and Robert Lowell. The following December, Bennoch sent another copy to Hall, who observed that

its proportions were identical to those of the other two Mayall photographs.

With characteristic enterprise and generosity, Bennoch had taken still another line of action: he arranged to have his recovered photograph copied in oils, lifesize, by the highly esteemed Scottish portrait painter Alexander Johnston (1815–1891). Previously, Bennoch had given a portrait bust of Longfellow to Bowdoin, and he now offered the college the "admirable" Hawthorne painting. In August 1886, as he told Holden, it was ready for shipment to America. Houghton had arranged to have it exhibited in Boston, where Bennoch learned it was well received, and it then went on to its home at Bowdoin. There, in the Hawthorne-Longfellow Library, it still hangs.

Bennoch's pleasure in the likeness of Hawthorne preserved in his photograph is evident in a letter he wrote in June 1887 responding to Hall's article on the Hawthorne photographs in the current *Athenaeum*. Agreeing with him that "the Bright picture & mine were doubtless taken on the same day," Bennoch firmly concluded, "I prefer my own."[17] Others who knew Hawthorne also praised it. George W. Curtis thought it was the best he had ever seen; his letter of 17 March 1886 thanked Holden for the "beautiful picture which is very much the most faithful and satisfactory likeness of Hawthorne as I remember him," and in the "Easy Chair" he called it a "remarkable likeness." The copy Holden later sent Julian—presumably at Bennoch's request—also elicited high, if qualified, praise. On 9 January 1887, Julian told Holden, "I consider it, if not the best, as good as the best that has been made of him; and with the other two English photos, presents as complete a picture of the man as photography can produce." Lathrop's praise in the *Century* the following April was equally high if equally qualified: he said the Bennoch "presents perhaps the truest and most comprehensive rendering of his personal appearance and of his individuality so far as it may be read upon the surface."

All of them got their copies from Holden, who obviously believed that the photograph was rightfully his

Oil painting by Alexander Johnston, 1886. Commissioned by Bennoch and presented to Bowdoin College. Photograph courtesy of Bowdoin College (opposite).

White-line wood engraving by Timothy Cole, 1887. In the *Century*.

property; and, indeed, Bennoch had said he held no copyright but controlled only prints from his new negative. Thus Holden felt free to offer his copy to *Harper's* and, after they refused it, to send it to the *Century*. His motives may be criticized, but an excellent engraved portrait of Hawthorne resulted from his initiative.

The *Century* readily accepted Holden's offer of the Bennoch photograph. On 13 August 1886, the editor wrote to thank Holden and to announce plans for engraving and publishing it:

In accepting this photograph for publication we made the promise to Mr. and Mrs. Lathrop that we would have it engraved in the highest style of the art and if possible by Mr. Cole, an engraver who is now employed in engraving the Old Masters for us in the European galleries. It is therefore impossible to hurry the work, and I am sorry to say that I cannot give a date when we can use the picture. If Mr. Cole consents to engrave it (which we are not sure that he will do) it will take a

great while as he is now in Italy. We will however see that it is engraved as soon as possible and will let you know when the date is fixed for publication.

"Mr. Cole" was Timothy Cole (1852–1931), a London-born artist who had come to this country in 1871 and worked for both the *Century* and *Scribner's*. He had developed a distinctive and recognizable style of white-line engraving, with a resourceful range of bold yet simple incisions that generated an effect of "calm and serene sureness."[18] He must have agreed to engrave the Hawthorne portrait almost immediately; perhaps he welcomed it as a change. He would spend a total of twenty-eight years in Italy engraving Old Masters for the *Century*.[19] His engraving of the entire "Bennoch" photograph was published as the frontispiece to the April 1887 issue of the *Century*, signed in the plate "T. Cole, Florence." Mayall is identified as the photographer and Bennoch as the owner. It was subsequently issued as Plate XXIII in the *Century Gallery of One Hundred Portraits* (New York: Century, 1897).

For that same issue of the *Century*, Lathrop wrote his extended essay on "Some Portraits of Hawthorne," first discussing the controversies about the other two Mayall photographs and then concentrating on Bennoch's. "A third English photograph—with the same costume, with one hand lying on a book upon a table, and the eyes looking straight forward (the face almost full)—has been brought to light within a few months," he said. According to Lathrop, "Francis Bennoch, another English friend of Hawthorne's—a wealthy manufacturer, member of Parliament, and amateur author, who figures frequently in the 'English Note-Books' and is still active in British politics,—had long cherished a photographic portrait, made in 1860, and presented to him by the romancer, which he esteemed the best one extant." Lathrop summarized the information Bennoch had given to Holden about how his photograph had been lost and then found, then reviewed facts about the various Mayall photographs and his own theories about Bright's and Motley's roles, concluding with Julian's statement of his certainty that Mayall took three separate poses.

Effectively this ended the controversy, at least in America, though Hall would have the last word in

Line engraving by Oliver Pelton, 1873. In the *Eclectic*.

Line engraving published by E. Dexter,1879. Courtesy of the National Portrait Gallery.

England a few months later. But curiously no one monitoring the Mayall portraits in the 1880s knew that the Bennoch pose had been engraved long before. Oliver Pelton (1798–1882), an artist famed for line-engraved portraits, prepared a rather stern-faced bust engraving of the Bennoch for the *Eclectic* magazine in 1873, and an unsigned engraving, copyright 1879, was published by the New York firm of E. Dexter. A copy is in the Library of Congress. We do not know how the engravers acquired the photograph. The image of Hawthorne in the composite oil painting and engraving of "Washington Irving and his Literary Friends at Sunnyside" (1863), both based on a drawing by F. O. C. Darley (1860), may perhaps be a reversed variant of the Bennoch pose, with the head inclined to the right and with a more sardonic expression than in the photograph (see pp. 112–14).

Other images followed the Cole engraving and the Johnston painting: an oil painting was made by the Massachusetts-born Alfred E. Smith (b. 1863), and a photoengraving of it, copyright 1898 by Foster Brothers of Boston, was published in this country and abroad. It appears in *Das Neunzehnte Jahrhundert in Bildnissen,* 1899, and in the *Outlook,* 1904. A copy of the Bennoch photograph in the Essex Institute collection made by Frank Cousins appears in the Salem *Proceedings.* Another oil portrait based on the Bennoch, done by the Iowa-born painter Charles Alden Gray (1857-1933), is in the Clark collection, and it is reproduced as the frontispiece for the *Nathaniel Hawthorne Journal 1973.*

The final published statement about the Mayall controversy, as well as the shortest and the most lucid, was Robert C. Hall's article, "The Photographs of Hawthorne," in the London *Athenaeum* on 18 June 1887. In it, Hall restated the problem and offered the solution he had summarized on the title page of his scrapbook—that three portraits were taken by Mayall on 19 May 1860 at Bright's request and with Hawthorne's knowledge and that Bright, Motley, and Bennoch each received a different pose. But Hall also ventured a personal judgment. He said that Bright's photograph "seems to me to best show his splendid eyes, full of thought or inspiration, as I have often seen him quietly walking along the streets of our city in his best moments."

Fields had called that same pose wonderful, and Sophia said it was noble and beautiful; Rose praised the "Holden" for capturing her father's characteristic mood of reverie, and Bennoch believed his own pose was the most characteristic of the lot. Yet there is no real dispute. Each of the remarkably detailed Mayall photographs captures a different facial angle. The Brady studios would take as many poses, and Boston photographers would take even more, but none with the Mayall blend of vitality and inwardness. Yet if we are to believe Elizabeth Peabody, these are photographs whose existence Hawthorne denied and which he probably never saw.

Notes

1. En route back to England from the continent, Hawthorne noted in his journal for 14 June that he did not know Bennoch's present address, "but I should deeply grieve to leave England without seeing him. He and Henry Bright are the only two men in England to whom I shall be much grieved to bid farewell..." (*FIN,* p. 570). Hawthorne wrote to Motley from Bath on 1 April 1860, saying that he intended to make a last visit to London and would "certainly come and see you." Motley died in 1877, Bright in 1884, and Bennoch in 1890.

2. Quoted by Julian Hawthorne, *NHW,* II: 258.

3. Ibid., II:257–58.

4. As ascertained by Robert C. Hall and recorded in his bound Scrapbook in the Berg Collection, New York Public Library. The title page of the scrapbook reads, "1886–1887 'Harper' & 'Century' Magazine's, with Portraits of Nath¹ Hawthorne's 'Photograph's, by Mayall 'of London'. With the absurd American Stories, & theories as to their *origin!* and all the original correspondence with *Mrs. H. A. Bright,—Mayall Jr.,* & *Francis Bennock,*—Hawthorne's London friend, all of which agree with Robert C. Hall's article in 'The Athenaeum'

of the 18 June, 1887. viz: as to their true origin,—all three having been taken by Mayall, on the —19th May 1860,—at the request of H. A. Bright of Liverpool— and as confirmed by Mrs. Bright, Mr. Mayall and Mr. Bennock &c., see their letters.—which also confute Mr. Holden's and Mr. Lathrop's articles in the two magazines of letters."

5. Gernsheim, pp. 292–303. See also Beaumont Newhall, *The Daguerreotype in America;* and William Welling, *Photography in America: The Formative Years, 1839–1900* (New York: Thomas Y. Crowell, 1978).

6. In his scrapbook, Hall included a letter from Bright's daughter dated 29 October 1886, in which she transcribed portions of letters sent to her father by Sophia Hawthorne and Fields and commented on the copies of the "Motley " print her father sent out.

7. Charles Henry Hart papers.

8. (New York: Oxford University Press, 1961).

9. "Biographical Sketch," pp. 561–62.

10. I am grateful to C. E. Frazer Clark, Jr., for allowing me to use Holden's file of letters, newspaper articles, and notes, now in the Clark collection, which also includes Holden's carte-sized vignette of the "Bright-Motley" pose and two cabinet-sized vignettes, nearly half-length, one of each "Holden" variant. Julian's understanding of English copyright law here was correct.

11. (Boston: Prang, 1886).

12. (Boston: Ticknor and Fields, 1866), facing p. 288.

13. As Buford Jones informs me, the image first appeared in James D. McCabe, Jr., *Great Fortunes and How They Were Made; or the Struggles and Triumphs of Our Self-Made Men* (Philadelphia: George MacLean, 1871), in Section 9, chapter 34, "Nathaniel Hawthorne," p. 579. The volume was reprinted in 1872, 1891, and 1972. The same portrait and narrative appeared in Walter R. Houghton, ed., *Kings of Fortune or The Triumphs and Achievements of Our Self-Made Men...* (Chicago: A. E. Davis, 1885), reprinted under various imprints in 1886, 1888, 1889, and 1890. The image is as reliable as the notion that Hawthorne, like Astor or Whitney, was one of America's "Kings of Fortune."

14. *NHW,* II:256–58.

15. *Visual Communication and the Graphic Arts: Photographic Technologies in the Nineteenth Century* (New York: R. R. Bowker, 1974), pp. 26, 58, 60. See

also Frank Luther Mott, *History of American Magazines,* III: 186–91.

16. I am grateful to Robert Nikirk, Librarian of the Grolier Club, for providing me with information about the medal and for showing me the d'Illzach model.

17. A carte copy was in Bennoch's papers sold at Sotheby's in 1976, but Sotheby's can provide no information about the disposition of the photograph or the papers. Bennoch's twenty-two letters to Holden, including his discussion of the Piercy episode and the Johnston portrait, are in the Francis Bennoch Collection of the Clifton Waller Barrett Library at the University of Virginia. Raymona Hull assumes that Bennoch did not pay the entire cost of the Johnston portrait but gathered a subscription for it. See her article on "Bennoch and Hawthorne," *Nathaniel Hawthorne Journal 1974,* p. 68.

18. Weitenkampf, pp. 134-35.

19. Mott, III:188, 472.

Mayall Chronology

1860   May: Bright and Hawthorne go to Mayall studios at 224 Regent Street, London. Mayall makes three negatives of Hawthorne. Bright chooses to have one of them printed. A second is printed and sent to Motley's residence. Bennoch comes to Mayall's with Hawthorne and chooses a third. All are printed in the large cabinet size, 6½ x 9 inches. Bright records the sitting in his diary. Mayall records only the copy sent to Motley. Mayall, Jr., later recalls Hawthorne looked like a Frenchman.

16 June: Hawthornes sail from Liverpool. According to Elizabeth Peabody's 1886 account, Sophia told her that on the steamship, Una praised the photograph of her father she had seen at Bright's house, but Hawthorne denied sitting for it and thought Una delirious.

Portrait by F. O. C. Darley made ca. 1860 (cf. *Sketches of Distinguished American Authors* [1863]), resembling Bennoch's image.

1864   19 May: Hawthorne dies.

21 August: Sophia writes to Bright requesting a copy of his photograph. Bright orders copy which he sends to Sophia.

5 November: Sophia writes to thank Bright for the "noble" picture. Fields requests a copy. Bright sends copies to him and to other Hawthorne admirers.

Hall reports in 1886 that an engraving based on the "Holden" appeared in an English edition of *Our Old Home* (London: Smith and Elder, 1864).

J. J. E. Mayall retires, succeeded by son.

1865   Hall acquires his Mayall carte of the "Holden." (Reported by Hall in 1886.)

Sophia's "Bright-Motley" engraved for *Good Company for Every Day in the Year.*

1867   Hall acquires his Mayall carte of the "Bright-Motley." (Reported by Hall in 1886.)

Mayall, Jr., reports commercial sale of Hawthorne portrait in various sizes "eight or ten years" after Hawthorne's death, though such sales began earlier. Photographers in England and America make and sell their own copies.

1871   February: Sophia dies. Her "Bright-Motley" photograph is passed on to her daughter Rose.

1872   Engraving based on "Bright-Motley" photograph published in *Harper's New Monthly Magazine.*

1873   Engraving by O. Pelton, based on "Bennoch" pose, appears in *Eclectic.*

1874   Julian Hawthorne acquires his Mayall carte of the "Bright-Motley" pose in London. (Reported by Julian in 1886.)

1877   Motley dies. His photograph passes on to his daughter.

1879   Engraving based on "Bennoch" photograph published by E. Dexter and Sons.

1880   Bennoch reports lending his photograph to Fred Piercy for a crayon drawing; photograph is misplaced in Piercy's studio until 1885.

1883   Lithograph by J. E. Baker based on "Bright-Motley" photograph published by Houghton Mifflin.

1884   Julian Hawthorne in *Nathaniel Hawthorne and His Wife,* II, retells Motley's "mythical" account in order to refute it and publishes both Bright's 1860 letter to Hawthorne and his recent letter to Julian recalling the Mayall sittings. Etching by S. A. Schoff based on Julian's Mayall carte included in volume.

1885   10 March: *Salem Gazette* publishes George H. Holden's account of Motley's version of the Mayall sitting, reported to him by Elizabeth Peabody.

15 April: Julian Hawthorne's brief letter to *Salem Gazette* insists "G. H. H.'s" account is wholly untrue.

Holden, to verify story, initiates correspondence with Mayall, Jr., Bennoch, and others.

Mayall, Jr., discovers father's "Holden" print and his father's record of mailing a copy to Motley. He copies the print for Holden.

Holden corresponds with *Harper's* editor, who arranges to engrave the "Holden" and requests an account of its supposed surreptitious origin for inclusion in the "Easy Chair."

Holden's correspondence with Francis Bennoch impels Bennoch to renew the issue of his missing photograph with Piercy. Bennoch has his photograph copied (later sending prints to Hall, Holden, and others).

1886   Bright dies. His photograph remains with his widow and daughter and is shown to Hall and Bennoch.

Alexander Johnston makes an oil painting based on Bennoch's photograph, exhibited in Boston, then sent to Bowdoin.

26 June: Julian Hawthorne again attacks Holden's "Motley" story in the New York *World.*

July: *Harper's* issue with engraving of "Holden" by Thomas Johnson as frontispiece, and W. H. Curtis's "Easy Chair," including Holden's revised account and new information from Mayall, Jr.

13 August: *Century* agrees to engrave Holden's copy of Bennoch's photograph.

21 August: Elizabeth Peabody's letter to the editor of *Salem Gazette,* published 31 August, gives Sophia's account of hearing about Bright's photograph and later acquiring a copy and defends Holden by giving Motley's account of surreptitiously arranging for that photograph with someone she concluded was not Mayall.

Robert C. Hall, determined to "set the record straight," communicates with Bright's widow, Mayall, Jr., and Bennoch. He begins assembling a scrapbook, to be concluded the following year. He learns from Mayall, Jr., about his father's favorite poses, his retouching practices, and exposure times.

Mayall, Jr., discovers his father's only surviving negative and makes prints for Hall, Holden, and others. He commissions a photogravure,

Bas relief by Edward J. Kuntze, 1860. The marble medallion—presented to Hawthorne in 1862—might have been destroyed after his death. The signed plaster cast was presented by Kuntze to the New-York Historical Society. Photograph courtesy of the New-York Historical Society.

but the plate is stolen and used for commercial catalogues.

1887   April: *Century Magazine* issue with engraving of "Bennoch" print by Timothy Cole as frontispiece and including G. P. Lathrop's lengthy article on "Some Portraits of Hawthorne."

           18 June: Hall's brief article on "The Photographs of Hawthorne" in London *Athenaeum* lays out the established facts, refuting the "absurd" accounts in *Harper's* and *Century*.

Bas Relief Medallion by Edward J. Kuntze (1860)

On 17 May 1860, the day after Hawthorne traveled from Bath to London for two weeks of social activity and travel, he wrote to Sophia, "Thou wouldst be stricken dumb to see how quietly I accept a whole string of invitations, and, what is more, perform my engage-

ments without a murmur." He then told her something even more surprising: "A little German artist has come to me with a letter of introduction, and a request that I will sit to him for a portrait in bas-relief. To this, likewise, I have assented!!!—subject to the condition that I shall have any leisure." The "little German artist" was Edward J. Kuntze (1826–1870), a sculptor and engraver born in Pomerania who was in America by 1852 and worked in Philadelphia and New York until his death, except for three years in London, from 1860 to 1863. Evidently, Hawthorne's disappointment with Louisa Lander's bust did not deter him from finding the leisure to sit for Kuntze, despite his crowded social schedule. Kuntze exhibited his 18½-inch marble bas relief medallion in London's Royal Academy Summer Exhibition of 1861 and was rewarded by having it praised and purchased.[1]

The *London Art-Journal* for December 1861 commented on the sculpture and on its artist:

A medallion of Hawthorne—one of the leading authors of America, and whose works, "The Scarlet Letter," and "The House of the Seven Gables," more especially, have achieved extensive popularity England [sic]—has been recently executed by an excellent sculptor, Küntze, of 23, Newman St. It was exhibited at the Royal Academy, and is a work of very great merit.

The *Journal* noted that "some friends and admirers of Hawthorne have arranged with the sculptor to present it to the lady of the estimable author," then went on to praise the author himself:

Mr. Hawthorne has many friends in England; particularly in Liverpool, where he was the American Consul—a post to which he was appointed solely on the ground of his abilities. Moreover, few men are more regarded and esteemed in private life. The testimonial, therefore, cannot fail to give pleasure to those who present, and to her who will receive it, while a well-deserved compliment will be paid to his friend the sculptor.[2]

In a letter to Hawthorne dated 14 February 1862, the English poet and novelist Berkeley Aikin spoke for more than three dozen subscribers who presented the bust to Hawthorne in recognition of his "genius." Her list includes Mr. Spiers and Mr. and Mrs. S. C. Hall (who appear in the Delamotte photograph of 1856) as well as Francis Bennoch, Kuntze, and herself. By August 1862, the marble medallion had reached Hawthorne at the Wayside by way of Salem. On 3 August, he addressed a letter to "Mr. Aikin" to thank his "friends and admirers" for sending it:

Both the medallion and letter have been very long in finding me out. Mr. Knight (whose letter enclosing yours, is dated May 2d) appears to have directed them to my native place at Salem, which for many years has ceased to be my home....I know not how to express to you and to those known and unknown friends...my deep sense of the honor that has been done me. When I look at this medallion I can almost fancy myself famous, since here is evidently a crystallization of the favorable judgments of men and women whose good opinion is most valuable—a solid and indestructible result, in marble, that has rewarded my poor literary attempts. I am well aware that the medallion will last till people shall have forgotten whose portraiture it is, and what were the works that seemed to your kindness to entitle me to such a testimonial...it will remain as an heirloom to my children, influencing them, I hope, to be prouder of their progenitor than he deserves.[3]

Although Hawthorne accepted the gift as a great compliment, he said nothing at all about the work of art itself. Nevertheless, the fact that he anticipated it would become a valued heirloom suggests at least that it did not displease him.

If Hawthorne gave the "solid and indestructible" medallion his tacit approval, Sophia did not. The *Art-Journal* was completely mistaken in thinking it could not "fail to give pleasure...to her who will receive it": she did not even consider it worthy of preservation. On 6 September 1868, shortly before her final departure from Concord, she wrote Rebecca Manning, "As we particularly wish the medallion should not be supposed a portrait of Mr. Hawthorne, being, as it is, so wretched a caricature of him, I will not burthen Richard with the weight of it. Loyalty to my husband seems to require it to be destroyed, but I do not know what we

shall decide to do with it."[4] Perhaps she did arrange to have it destroyed, though possibly Hawthorne's cousin Richard Clarke Manning appropriated it, along with other family possessions.

George Parsons Lathrop's comments on the medallion in his "Biographical Sketch" clearly indicate he had seen it, and, on the whole, it pleased him as an index of Hawthorne's appearance at the end of his "European life":

He allowed a thick mustache to grow, during his last stay in England, and it was then that Kuntze modelled his profile, which sets Hawthorne's features before us in a totally different way from any of the other portraits. Unfortunately, Kuntze's relief is reduced to a size below that of life, and the features accordingly assume a cramped relation. The lofty forehead is given its due importance, however, and concentration of impassioned energy is conveyed by the outline of the face, from this point of view. The chin, always forcible as well as delicate, impresses one in this case with a sense of persistent and enduring determination on the part of the original; and with this sense there is mingled an impression of something that approaches sternness, caused, it may be, by the hirsute upper lip. (p. 560)

Lathrop seems to be commenting on the original marble medallion, an indication that Sophia did not destroy it in 1868. But it is conceivable that he saw a plaster version. In 1868, Kuntze presented his own framed plaster copy of the medallion—signed at the bottom "E. Kuntze, Sculp."—to the New-York Historical Society, and there it still remains, dated (incorrectly) "c. 1865–68."[5]

The medallion has special interest as the last sculpted likeness of Hawthorne, and (like the Mayall photographs) as a record of Hawthorne's appearance at the end of his stay in England, but it has intrinsic merit as well. We can speculate about why Sophia considered it a caricature; perhaps she was repelled by the receding hairline, the prominent nose, the retracted lower lip, the weak and sagging chin, or the sinuous curls at the back of Hawthorne's head. To Lathrop the chin suggested determination, but even though the upper profile carries that suggestion, the line from the chin to the neck conveys an impression of slackness. Nevertheless, the eye is delicately molded, and the curved spray of Hawthorne leaves and blossoms at the bottom is at once a witty and aesthetically appropriate complement to the famous flowing locks, strong brow, deep-set eyes, and full moustache.

Notes

1. The work is listed as #998 in the Royal Academy catalogue, as I was first informed by Elizabeth A. Evans, Research Consultant of the National Portrait Gallery in London.

2. The commentary appears in the *Art-Journal,* 7 (December 1861): 351, under the heading "Minor Topics of the Month."

3. I am indebted to Neal Smith for transcripts of the Aikin letter and Hawthorne's reply. Berkeley Aikin was the pseudonym of Fanny Aikin Kortright, an English poet and novelist. Mr. Knight was possibly Charles Knight, publisher of a series of guides to London.

4. Essex Institute manuscript.

5. I am grateful to Richard J. Koke, Curator of the New-York Historical Society, for showing me the medallion and providing a photograph of it. It is listed as #334 in the *Catalogue of American Portraits in the New-York Historical Society* (1974), p. 131, which gives the date of "c. 1865–68."

Later American Portraits

"[Hawthorne] was several times painted and photographed, but it was impossible for art to give the light and beauty of his wonderful eyes."

(Fields, **Yesterdays with Authors**, p. 41)

Family Sketches of Nathaniel Hawthorne (1861)

Two very similar bust pencil sketches of Hawthorne's left profile are in the Berg Collection, one by Una and one by Julian, both done in Concord in 1861, probably in the sitting room of the Wayside. Both show Hawthorne in his familiar dark jacket, high-collared shirt, and bow tie, seated in an easy chair. As in the Kuntze profile medallion, the hairline has markedly receded, the moustache droops, and the chin seems weak and sagging, especially by contrast to the salient nose.

Una's sketch—laid into Rose's album—is mounted in an oval cardboard frame, 4½ x 3½ inches, with double pencil ruling. Working with a well-sharpened hard pencil, Una took special pains to define her father's curling hair and double chin. Julian's drawing is about the same size on a 5 x 7 sheet on whose verso is a sketch done along the Massachusetts seashore, presumably also by him. Working with a softer pencil and in a position slightly to the right of Una's, Julian showed his father reading a book (lightly indicated), and he carefully rendered details of the jacket, the chair back, and background shadows. But the posture and clothing are the same in both, and the locks of hair curl in exactly the same way, particularly over the ear. Possibly both drawings were produced in the course of the same evening.

A third small pencil sketch, perhaps made on the same occasion, is included in the family album owned by Manning Hawthorne (the album that also includes the pencil sketch by Sophia, perhaps the one she did of Hawthorne in 1838; see p. 19). This drawing shows part of a right profile—the right eye and brow, a firm nose, a sagging cheek, and the top hairs of a moustache. The cross-hatchings around the eye and the deftly modeled nose are clearly the work of a more accomplished draftsman than either Una or Julian, and the brief sketch conveys an impression of earnest thought missing from the two penciled busts. It is nice to conjecture that Sophia made this drawing, sitting on her husband's right, while Julian and Una sketched him from the left, fixing the patriarchal features. It would be wholly in keeping with Sophia's concentration on her husband's eternal rather than temporal image that she would concentrate on his eyes and ignore his hairline, his chinline, and his clothing; however, the downward lines of the cheek and the downswing of the eyebrow do record the onset of age.

Photograph of Nathaniel and Sophia Hawthorne in Concord (1861?)

Nathaniel and Sophia Hawthorne appear as small figures in the lower left of a photograph displaying their Concord home, the Wayside, after additions were completed in December 1860. The photograph shows the tower study and the chimney tops constructed after the Hawthornes returned from England. Husband and wife stand in their eight-acre lot situated across the Boston Road from the house, hats on as if for a walk, Hawthorne holding Sophia's left arm while his own left arm is slightly bent and behind him. Judging by the unbudded trees and the fact that Mrs. Hawthorne is wearing only a dress without an outer garment (as well as the existence of another photograph which

Pencil sketch by Una Hawthorne, 1861. Laid into Rose Hawthorne Lathrop's album of photographs and family memorabilia. Courtesy of the Henry W. and Albert A. Berg Collection, The New York Public Library.

shows the west wing of the house, unbudded trees, and Sophia in the same dress), the picture might have been one of several taken on a mild day in the early spring of 1861 to record changes in the Wayside.[1]

Julian Hawthorne included a copy of this photograph in *Hawthorne and His Circle* (1903), and several later publications of it indicate that Julian copyrighted the photograph that year. Most reproductions of the image are probably copies from Julian's volume. The National Park Service in Concord has a copy of the photograph, but with no information about its origin.

Notes

1. See Anna Coxe Toogood, *The Wayside Historic Grounds Report* (Washington, D.C.: United States Department of the Interior, 1970); and Robert D. Ronsheim,

Pencil sketch by Julian Hawthorne, 1861. Courtesy of the Henry W. and Albert A. Berg Collection, The New York Public Library.

The Wayside Historic Structure Report Part II, Historical Data Section (Washington, D.C.: United States Department of the Interior, 1968), both of which reproduce these photographs.

Boston Photographs (1861–1862)

When Hawthorne left America for England in July 1853, dozens of daguerreotypists were in business along Washington Street. By the time he returned (June 1860), the studios had converted to the newer forms of photography, primarily the wet collodion process; and advertisements in the *Boston City Directories* promised a wide range of options and services.

After his return, Hawthorne was photographed on at least three separate occasions in the best known of the galleries on Washington Street. Two and possibly

Pencil sketch probably by Sophia Hawthorne, 1861(?). In the Hawthorne family album owned by Manning Hawthorne.

1862; and the firm is listed at the same address as Case and Getchell in 1863 and 1864. They ran a large advertisement each of those years, in 1861 listing the names of G. M. Silsbee and J. G. Case but also W. H. Getchell. The ad announced "Photographs and Daguerreotypes taken in the highest perfection of the art" and promised that "duplicate photographs can be supplied at any time." The longer advertisement the following year elaborated on the consumer's options. It announced "Photographs of all sizes, from Miniature to Life Size, and finished in INDIA INK, OIL, WATER, AND PASTILLE COLORS," and specified, "We are paying particular attention to the very popular picture 'carte de visite.'" In *The Camera and The Pencil* (1864), the first major historical account of photography in the United States, the contemporary photographer Marcus Aurelius Root observed, "Messrs. Case & Getchell, successors to Measury & Silsby, of Boston, have also a large and popular establishment in that city," and he offered high praise: "Their cartes de visite and larger photographs are, for beauty and artistic effect, surpassed by few if by any."[1]

Seated Pose by W. H. Getchell

When Hawthorne walked upstairs at 299½ Washington St. to sit for his portrait, the photographer was W. H. Getchell. Getchell is identified as the superintendent of the photography department in a pamphlet the firm published in 1858, *The Greatest Triumph of Modern Art*.[2] The pamphlet delineates "the history and progress of photography," culminating in the firm's studios, with Case as supervisor. Silsbee is identified as the colorist, a skillful artist with "a most extensive practice in every branch of the painter's art," who "superintends the coloring department, assisted by artists eminent as himself." Getchell is praised as a man of great ability whose fine reputation came "from a long connection with this establishment as its Principle Photographic Operator."

Precise identification of Getchell as the photographer of Hawthorne comes from George Parsons Lathrop's article on the Hawthorne portraits, where he cites Getchell as an authority on the minimum time required for taking photographs at this time. Lathrop identified him

three photographs were taken by W. H. Getchell of the firm of Silsbee and Case, five or six by the celebrated photographer James Wallace Black, and possibly one or more by John Adams Whipple. One of the Silsbee and Case photographs is particularly well known through versions in other media: a drawing, engravings, a gold-stamped image on a series of book covers, an oil painting, and a statue. Two of the Black photographs have been reproduced—slightly different poses of Hawthorne standing between his publishers Ticknor and Fields—and several quite different bust engravings seem based on the photograph known as the "Field Marshal." The other Boston photographs are relatively unknown.

Silsbee and Case

The firm of Silsbee, Case, and Getchell did business under slightly different names during Hawthorne's last years. Listings and advertisements for Silsbee and Case at 299½ Washington St., "up but one flight of stairs," appear in the *Boston Directories* for 1860, 1861, and

Photograph of Nathaniel and Sophia Hawthorne at their Concord home, the Wayside, 1861, after their return from England. First pub-lished by Julian Hawthorne in *Hawthorne and His Circle* (1903).

as "Mr. Getchell (a partner of Silsbee, Case & Co., who made an excellent photograph of Hawthorne in 1861–62, engraved for THE CENTURY of May, 1886)."

The "excellent photograph" Lathrop referred to is the best known of the Boston photographs and the one with the largest progeny. It is a three-quarter-length photograph showing Hawthorne seated, turned to the left but looking forward, wearing a double-breasted velvet-collared jacket, a shirt with a stand-up collar, and a shawl-collared great coat, and holding in his left hand a large-brimmed soft-crowned hat. The hat might well be the one Rose Hawthorne Lathrop referred to when describing her father's habits "in 1861 and thereafter" in "My Father's Literary Methods": "He wore a soft, brown felt hat, and looked in it like a brother to Tennyson, though with a difference," she

said.[3] This is probably the same "soft brown felt hat" he had acquired abroad and wore there along with what is probably the coat in the photograph, "a brown Talma of finest broadcloth" that had an artistic "double-decked" effect.[4] If so, this is probably the first portrait in which Hawthorne is not wholly garbed in black.

It is also the only one of the Boston photographs for which we are offered a precise date: 19 December 1861, over three months before Hawthorne was photo-graphed in the studio of Mathew Brady. This is the date given on an autotype from the original reproduced as the frontispiece to Wallace Hugh Cathcart's *Bibliography of the Works of Nathaniel Hawthorne*,[5] and the date accepted by both the National Portrait Gallery and the Frick Art Reference Library. The carte-sized copy tipped into Rose Hawthorne Lathrop's photo-graph album on the bottom of page 9 might be a print

Hawthorne once owned, and both the date and the pose suggest that Hawthorne sent his friend Horatio Bridge another carte copy of the same photograph on 13 February 1862, declining Bridge's invitation to visit Washington. Hawthorne wrote, "Meanwhile, I send you, enclosed, a respectable old gentlemen who, my friends say, is very like me and may serve as my representative."

It seems likely that Hawthorne's approval reflected Sophia's. In a letter to James T. Fields on 1 January 1862 she spoke of three photographs taken at the "urgent request" of Silsbee and Case.

You would have been filled with admiration of my lord, if you had witnessed the celestial patience with which he allowed the photographer to poke about his sacred face and figure, arranging even the hairs of his head and almost his eyelashes, and turning his brow as if on a pivot. He was as docile as the dearest baby, though he hates to be touched any more than anyone I ever knew.

Sophia complained about the duration of the sittings, which seemed "the cunningest torture invented by man." She also complained about the photograph of the children taken that day, and her own seemed "frightful." But one of the three portraits made by the fussy photographer who was "not so quick as Whipple" pleased her enormously. "One of the pictures is very bad, and one he has not sent," she told Fields; "but I forgive him for all his sins since he has brought out this perfect one." Delighted that Silsbee and Case had presented her with several copies of the "perfect" picture, she enclosed one as a New Year's gift for Fields, certain he would "like it better than any other present."

It would always remain one of her favorite portraits of her husband. A letter she sent him in April 1862, near the end of his Washington visit, expresses her pleasure in a neighbor's response. "At the Old Manse Mrs Ripley said she had seen the card photograph by Getchell in Mr Bradford's book and she never saw anything so beautiful as a picture or as a man!"[6] Soon after Hawthorne's death, in June 1864, acknowledging receipt of another photograph from Fields, she commented on her pleasure in the portrait "with a hat"

Photograph by W. H. Getchell of Silsbee and Case, 1861. Courtesy of C. E. Frazer Clark, Jr.

(probably this one) saying she had loved it "so long, I am jealous of having it replaced."

The card photograph probably went on sale soon after Sophia received her prints, and several have survived: two are in Clark's collection—one with the "Silsbee, Case & Co." imprint and a later one with "Case & Getchell." Other photographers in Boston and elsewhere also produced copies, such as the one John Robinson of Salem sent Charles Henry Hart on 7 April

Line engraving by J. A. J. Wilcox, 1883. Frontispiece to twelfth volume of the Riverside Edition of Hawthorne's works.

Crayon drawing by Samuel W. Rowse, 1865. Photographic copy courtesy of the Longfellow National Historic Trust.

1898. "You spoke of not having the hat in the print of the Hawthorne photograph," Robinson wrote. "On looking into the matter I found where the negative is and had a full length made which I enclose." He added the few facts he had learned about it: "The story is that it was enlarged from a small carte photograph or ambrotype taken by Silsbee and Case in Boston." The information is restated on the back of Hart's photograph, with a notation that the copy negative was owned by W. G. Hussey of Salem.[7] The Clark collection includes a cabinet print with Hussey's name at the bottom.

A year and a half after Hawthorne died, Fields commissioned the well-known artist Samuel Worcester Rowse (1822–1901) to do a crayon drawing based on the photograph. Rowse, who also did engraving and

lithography in Boston between 1852 and 1872, was especially renowned for black crayon portraits. On 20 November 1865, Sophia asked Fields, "Is Mr. Rowse using my picture? Is he succeeding in making a likeness?" Rowse's drawing became one of Fields's favorite portraits, and Sophia considered it "a miracle."

After both she and Rose had seen the completed work, Sophia wrote on 12 September 1866 to tell Fields how strongly it affected them both:

Rose was struck blind (as I was giddy) when she first looked at the portrait. But when she got home she said there was a want—she believed it was lack of sweetness and radiance of expression—but something. But she says it is a miracle that Mr. Rowse has performed—as it is—I wish I could bless you in some way, but I can't.[8]

Surely Sophia was right about the "lack of sweetness" in the Rowse drawing; Hawthorne looks solemn, as he did in the photograph on which it was based. Lathrop's brief comment in his "Biographical Sketch" concentrates on that solemnity, "that sturdy, almost military, resoluteness so marked in the familiar crayon portrait by Rowse, executed after Hawthorne's return from Italy and England" (pp. 558–59).

Fields, however, thought the Rowse was both "exquisite" and "truthful." His discussion of Hawthorne in *Yesterdays with Authors* begins with an image that becomes the unifying device of the chapter: "I am sitting to-day opposite the likeness of the rarest genius America has given to literature.... The portrait I am looking at was made by Rowse (an exquisite drawing), and is a very truthful representation of the head of Nathaniel Hawthorne." Fields did have one criticism, but it applied to all portraits of Hawthorne: "He was several times painted and photographed, but it was impossible for art to give the light and beauty of his wonderful eyes." Fields returned to the image of himself as spectator to introduce a later section of his chapter, saying, "Hawthorne is still looking at me in his far-seeing way, as if he were pondering what was next to be said about him." And Fields began his last section with a broader comment about how the drawing affected him: "Whenever I look at Hawthorne's portrait, and that is pretty often, some new trait or anecdote or reminiscence comes up and clamors to be made known to those who feel an interest in it" (pp. 41, 64, 101).[9]

Annie Fields must have inherited the Rowse drawing after her husband's death in 1881. The photocopy of the vignetted bust published as the frontispiece to the Salem *Proceedings* is identified as "From the crayon portrait made by Samuel Rowse in 1866, now in possession of Mrs. Annie Fields, Boston, Mass." The copy in the Frick Art Reference Library collection is attributed "Courtesy of Mrs. Charles Henry Hart," suggesting that in the course of Hart's investigations of Hawthorne portraits, he might have acquired the Rowse and bequeathed it to his wife.

Soon after the Rowse drawing was made, Longfellow had acquired his own photographic copy of it, an albumen print measuring 8⅞ x 6⅞ inches, mounted on a cream-colored mat rounded at the top and edged with two gilt lines. A photograph from around 1870 shows it hanging in the side hall on the first floor of Craigie House, where it hangs today. It is probably Longfellow's photograph of the Rowse drawing that Howells recalled in "My First Visit to New England" as the picture he had noticed while dining with Longfellow: "When one of the guests happened to speak of the photograph of Hawthorne which hung in a corner of the room, Lowell said, after a glance at it, 'Yes, it's good; but it hasn't his fine *accipitral* look.'"[10]

The Longfellow photograph of the Rowse drawing seems to be identical to the one Julian Hawthorne used as the frontispiece to *Hawthorne and His Circle*. The image in the Salem *Proceedings* is almost imperceptibly different; perhaps it was made from a later photograph. Another slightly more detailed vignette prepared for commercial distribution was copyrighted in 1901 by the A. W. Elson Company. The Library of Congress retains a copy negative.

Perhaps Fields communicated his fondness for his Rowse drawing to Houghton and Mifflin. The volumes of the Fireside Edition (1879–1882) have a similar image goldstamped on the front cover and a small engraving of it on the title page. The same Silsbee and Case image was engraved for the Riverside Edition (1883–1891) by John Angel James Wilcox (1835–aft. 1913), an artist who worked in Boston from 1860 on and was particularly admired for his line-engraved portraits. His Hawthorne portrait, signed at the right shoulder "J. A. J. Wilcox, Boston," appears as the frontispiece to the Riverside Edition's twelfth volume. Together with the other illustrations for this edition it was included in the *Hawthorne Portfolio* of 1883 and the deluxe edition of 1884; the publishers advertised it as "a new Portrait from the best photograph in the possession of the family." Examples can be found in the print collections of the Library of Congress and the University of Virginia, among others. The engraving was included in the *Critic*'s Hawthorne issue of July 1904, with the credit line "Courtesy of Houghton Mifflin," and the (incorrect) identification "HAWTHORNE AT THE AGE OF SIXTY," and it was also published in *Moulton's Library of Criticism* (1904).

A bust engraving similar to the one by Wilcox, but combining stipple with line engraving, was made by

Line engraving by Hezekiah Wright Smith. Courtesy of the Baltimore Museum of Art.

Hezekiah Wright Smith, perhaps at the same time or a few years earlier. A copy hangs in the Baltimore Museum of Art, mounted together with a Smith portrait of Longfellow—both, according to the museum card, 85 x 65 mm, on laid China paper—and the National Portrait Gallery owns another copy of Smith's Hawthorne. Smith (1828–aft. 1879) had worked in Boston in 1850 with Joseph Andrews (the engraver of Sophia's Ilbrahim), then moved to New York and Philadelphia, winning fame for his engravings of famous writers and statesmen (particularly for his head of Washington, copied from the *Athenaeum* portrait). According to Weitenkampf (pp. 82, 95), he was one of the "nimble manipulators" who "flooded the land with portraits" in response to commercial demand, making effective use of the mixed method of engraving.

At least one other distinguished stipple and line engraving was produced at the end of the century—a nearly half-length engraving, 19½ x 14½ inches, done by the medal-winning French artist Henri Emile Lefort

(b. 1852) a Chevalier of the Legion of Honor. Copies are hanging at the Grolier Club and the Baltimore Museum of Art. In the middle of the lower margin, a decorative letter A is imprinted above the identification "NATHANIEL HAWTHORNE (about 1862)," with images of two Puritan men at the left and Hester with Pearl in her lap at the right.

The "excellent photograph of Hawthorne in 1861–62" made by Getchell was indeed "engraved for THE CENTURY of May, 1886," as Lathrop noted in his 1887 *Century* article. The unsigned white-line wood engraving of the entire photograph dominates the concluding page of Julian Hawthorne's article on "Hawthorne's Philosophy," identified as "Nathaniel Hawthorne (about 1862). (From a photograph by Sillsbee, Case & Co. [*sic*].)" The fact that an unsigned white-line engraving of the Whipple daguerreotype appeared as frontispiece in the same issue, with the artist identified as Thomas Johnson, suggests at least the possibility that Johnson also engraved the photograph.

In 1893, an oil painting based on the well-known Getchell image was made by H. Frances Osborne as a gift for the Essex Institute. The canvas, measuring 30 x 21 inches, shows Hawthorne with heavy gray hair but a dark moustache and holding a gray hat. A photomechanical copy was issued by the A. W. Elson Company as a separate print, later published in the Salem *Proceedings*.

The full-length bronze statue of Hawthorne on Hawthorne Boulevard in Salem has as its origin the same Getchell photograph. The sculptor commissioned by the Hawthorne Memorial Association was Bela Lyon Pratt (1867–1917), a student of Saint Gaudens, whose work includes the statue of Nathan Hale at Yale, "The Seasons" in the Library of Congress, and many memorial statues. The Hawthorne statue, cast by the Gorham Company, was dedicated on 23 December 1925.

Seated Pose, Profile, by W. H. Getchell

A seated half-length photograph showing Hawthorne in profile, looking right, may be the Getchell pose that seemed "very bad" to Sophia. Hawthorne is wearing what seems to be the same clothing as in the "perfect" pose but with the overcoat removed—a double-breasted,

White-line wood engraving perhaps by Thomas Johnson, 1886. Illustration for Julian Hawthorne's article on "Hawthorne's Philosophy" in the *Century*.

Bronze statue by Bela Pratt, 1925. On Hawthorne Boulevard in Salem.

velvet-collared coat and a shirt with a high collar. The moustache seems equally bushy in both pictures, but here the cheeks seem sunken. The hypothesis that both photographs were made in the same studio is supported by a copy in the Clark collection: the back of the photograph has the Case and Getchell imprint, as well as the inscribed name of Annie Fields. A vignetted copy of the same photograph, also in Clark's collection, is tantalizingly inscribed on the back, "Elizabeth from Anne," though with no indication as to which Elizabeth received it from which Anne. This pose is probably the one Julian mentioned in the letter Lathrop quoted in his *Century* article on Hawthorne's portraits

Line engraving by Henri E. Lefort. Courtesy of the Baltimore Museum of Art (opposite).

as showing "Hawthorne seated, in profile, three-quarters length" and taken in "1861–2 [*sic*]."

The entire photograph was later copied by the Salem firm of A. C. Mackintire. The image in the Salem *Proceedings* is identified as taken from Mackintire's copy, made around 1891, from "a photograph probably taken in Boston around 1862–63." A cabinet copy with the Mackintire imprint is at the Essex Institute.

Seated Pose

Another three-quarter-length photograph shows Hawthorne seated on a chair that is turned to the left. He is turned to the right and looking forward. This time he is wearing a single-breasted, velvet-collared coat and a loosely tied cravat. His left hand rests on his knee,

Photograph by W. H. Getchell of Silsbee and Case, 1861. Courtesy of C. E. Frazer Clark, Jr.

Photograph by Silsbee and Case, perhaps by W. H. Getchell, 1861. Courtesy of Barbara Bacheler.

and his right hand is bent, resting on the back of the chair, loosely holding the same broad-brimmed hat as in the picture Rowse copied. A carte in the Clark collection bears the Case and Getchell imprint on the back; and Hawthorne's hair seems as gray and the moustache as full as in the two photographs with Silsbee and Case imprints.

The carte reproduced here is one of three given by the Hawthornes to Dora Golden and passed on to her

descendants. Dora had been the family's nursemaid in Salem from 1846 to 1850, and a friendly relationship continued even after Hawthorne's death. The second of Dora's photographs is of Sophia alone, with the Silsbee and Case imprint on the back; and the third is of Una, Julian, and Rose, showing the same rug as in the photograph of Sophia.[11] It seems certain that all three of Dora's photographs were taken by Silsbee and Case, perhaps on the same day. The photographs of

Photograph of Sophia Hawthorne by Silsbee and Case, 1861. Courtesy of Barbara Bacheler.

Photograph of Una, Julian, and Rose Hawthorne by Silsbee and Case, 1861. Courtesy of Barbara Bacheler.

the three children and of Sophia might be the ones she criticized in her letter to Fields of 1 January 1862, and the session at the Silsbee studio might have been the one anticipated in her letter to Annie Fields dated 8 December 1861:

And this week I go again with every one of the Hawthorne flowers to be photographed for a very dear elderly lady, who is on her death-bed, but with love for her beloved so vivid still, that she is collecting them all *into her beautiful clasped volume to hold in her hand and look at until her eyes close on mortal life. No other circumstances could have persuaded me to be photographed.*[12]

Thus it seems likely that all the photographs given to Dora were taken in mid-December 1861. It is even conceivable that all three of the photographs of Hawthorne in this group were made on the same occasion; the fussy Getchell might have asked Hawthorne to arrange for a change of clothing. If so, this third seated pose might be the one the photographer did not at first send to Sophia.

A number of card-sized prints have survived (some of them pirated). An albumen print is tipped into copy 5 of *The Scarlet Letter* in the Berg Collection, and a mounted print is at the Essex Institute.

James Wallace Black

Five or six photographs of Hawthorne were taken in the Washington Street studios of one of the most famous Boston photographers, James Wallace Black. On the evidence of Hawthorne's clothing and hair, as well as the marble column in the background, five were taken in the same place and at the same time. Three are of Hawthorne alone, two seated and one standing, and two show him standing between his publishers, William B. Ticknor and James T. Fields. Hawthorne appears to be wearing the same clothing in each: a double-breasted coat with an overcoat on top, a bow-tied stock, and a shirt with a standing white collar; and all the standing poses show him with a top hat.

At the time Hawthorne visited his studios, James Wallace Black (1825–1896) was widely recognized as a prominent figure in the development of American photography. Marcus Aurelius Root said in *The Camera and The Pencil* that "Black was noted for his extraordinary energy and skill" and that "Mr. Black's success for the last five years in all branches of his profession, is probably without a parallel in the United States at this date (1863)." Noting the size of Black's establishment, employing over sixty men and women, Root concluded, "The excellent specimens here produced, coupled with his energy and courteous deportment, have placed him where he now stands,—in the forefront of the profession."[13] Today Black is best known for making the first American aerial photograph, a picture of Boston taken from a balloon. As Welling notes, Black also introduced the porcelain photograph, in partnership with the same Case who had previously been in partnership with Silsbee and Getchell.[14]

Black's advertisements in the *Boston City Directory* during Hawthorne's last years are large and detailed. The advertisement for the firm listed as Black and Batchelder in the 1861 *Directory* defines a wide range of options for "Photographs taken in every style" under a "ground-glass skylight" and promises to preserve negatives for future duplication. Customers were invited to order "Copies made from Small Daguerreotypes, Ambrotypes, or Melanotypes, and enlarged to any size, either plain, finished in India Ink, or Colors. Also, life-sized Photographs taken on canvas, finished in oil colors," all done "by the best artists." Black's expansive advertisement for 1864 gives the range of prices at his "well-known establishment,... varying in accordance with the style and finish, from the 'Carte de Visite' at $4 per dozen to the 'Life Size' in oil at $50 to $125."

Although it is not certain that Black was .himself behind the camera when Hawthorne came into his establishment with Ticknor and Fields, it seems likely that the energetic proprietor would have claimed that privilege. The photographs were probably taken with one of Black's multi-lens carte de visite cameras, and similarities between each of the two group pictures and each of the two seated poses suggest that they were taken only seconds apart. Although we cannot know how much Black was paid, nor by whom, the price of four dollars per dozen was apparently the standard price for cartes.

A possible date for the entire group of photographs is suggested by an imprint on a carte copy of one of the seated poses in the Clark Collection: "Photographed by Black and Batchelder, 173 Washington St., Boston." That is how the firm is listed in the *Boston Directory* for the year beginning 1 July 1861. The 1860 *Directory* had listed Batchelder alone at that address, and the 1861 advertisement for Black and Batchelder specified that Black had previously been in business with Whipple. The *Directories* for 1862, 1863, and 1864 list only Black at that address (and in 1863 and 1864 also at 163 Washington Street, suggesting an increase in business). In 1865, the name of Case is added. The Black and Batchelder imprint thus suggests that Clark's carte and the four others in the same group were taken during a visit to Black's studio between July 1860 and June 1862 and that copies which bear the imprints of Black alone or of Black and Case were made subsequently from negatives Black had retained. They might have been taken shortly before Hawthorne left for Washington

Photograph by James Wallace Black, 1861 or 1862. Courtesy of C. E. Frazer Clark, Jr.

Photograph by James Wallace Black, 1861 or 1862. Courtesy of the Massachusetts Historical Society.

with Ticknor on 7 March 1862. Although Julian's recollection was often faulty, his letter to Lathrop dates the carte of Hawthorne with his two publishers as 1861–1862 and specifies that it preceded the Washington trip.

Seated Poses

Clark's Black and Batchelder carte is a full-length pose showing Hawthorne seated to the right of a table, with a column to the right behind him. He is turned half right, his feet separated, with the right foot in front, his left arm resting loosely on the arm of the chair. In his right hand he is holding a small book, apparently reading it. This same pose was published in the Salem *Proceedings* and attributed to the firm of Black and Case; it is listed as "in possession of the Misses Manning, Salem, Mass." The standing pose in that volume has the same attribution and is listed as "in possession of Mrs. Rebecca C. Manning, Salem, Mass.," suggesting that members of the Manning family acquired both prints when the firm was known as Black and Case, i.e., after Hawthorne's death.

A second, almost identical, seated pose has never, to my knowledge, been published, although two copies have survived in the collections of the Massachusetts Historical Society, evidence of the fashion of collecting

Photograph by James Wallace Black, 1861 or 1862. Courtesy of the Massachusetts Historical Society.

Standing Pose

In the three-quarter-length standing photograph of Hawthorne alone, Hawthorne's body is to the camera but his head and eyes are turned half right; his left arm is bent and rests loosely on the base of the column, and he holds a top hat in his lowered right hand. A card-sized print is pasted into an album owned by the Massachusetts Historical Society.[15] That copies were not limited to those printed by Black (such as the Manning family's print reproduced in the Salem *Proceedings*) is confirmed by John Robinson's letter to Charles Henry Hart of 7 April 1898, enclosing a print made by A. C. Mackintire of Salem. After commenting on his acquisition of the Silsbee and Case pose that Rowse had used, Robinson said, "Also I send another (and if you like Hawthorne's hats here is a funny old one) which was copied from a card photograph owned by a Mr. Carleton or Carlton of Boston. Mrs. Frank Cousin...lent me the negatives from which these prints were made."[16]

The bronze bust of Hawthorne made by Daniel Chester French for New York University's Hall of Fame seems based on this photograph: in both, Hawthorne is wearing a lapelled greatcoat over a double-breasted coat whose collar is loosely opened, revealing a knotted stock and high collar, and his expression is meditative. French might have drawn on other late photographs as well, however, in which Hawthorne's cheeks are similarly sunken, the eyes lined, and the expression somber. French (1850–1931) studied in Boston under William Rimmer, completing his first commission, the Concord Minuteman, at twenty-three. His best-known works include a bust of Emerson at Harvard and the statue of Lincoln in the Lincoln Memorial in Washington, D.C. His bust of Hawthorne was unveiled in May 1929 by Hawthorne's granddaughter Una Hawthorne Deming, as a gift from an 1899 Bowdoin graduate, L. B. Leavitt. A plaster copy, 31¼ inches high and signed on the left side "D. C. French Sc.," was given by the sculptor's daughter to the New-York Historical Society in 1953; it appears as #891 in their *Catalogue of Portraits* (p. 341).

carte photographs of celebrities. The first is a card without an imprint; the second is a card bearing on the back the imprint of Black at 163 Washington St. and mounted in a folder together with a letter to Fields. This suggests that possibly Fields had once owned the photograph itself. This second seated pose is essentially like the first, even to the placement of the feet. But here the right hand is resting on the table and loosely grasping the small book; the eyes are now lowered and gazing ahead; and a cloth object that had been on the table in the first pose has vanished.

Bronze bust by Daniel Chester French, 1929. In the Hall of Fame (opposite).

Hawthorne with Ticknor and Fields

Two quite separate full-length poses of Hawthorne and his publishers have survived, although Lathrop's description of the group in his 1887 *Century* article on Hawthorne's portraits, as well as Julian's quoted comment, indicate they both assumed only one such group photograph existed:

Mr. Julian Hawthorne, in a letter to me, speaks of "a carte-de-visite of Fields, Hawthorne, and Ticknor in a group, full length and standing, with their hats on." This curious little souvenir, depicting Hawthorne and his publishers as they appeared in every-day life, on the streets of Boston or in the Old Corner Bookstore, is quite rare. It has never been engraved. Mr. Bennoch, having lately seen a copy of it, referred to it in a private letter as "a portrait of those tall hats. The heads," he added, "and the grouping, remind me of a group of old Jews at the corner of Petticoat Lane, haggling over some recent purchase of 'old clo'.' It may be appreciated by the curiosity-hunter, but never by those who loved the originals." I think, however, that Mr. Bennoch underrates the value of this unique transcript from the life. What would we not give to-day for some similar representation of Shakspere hobnobbing with Ben Johnson at the Mermaid Tavern, engaging in a "wit-combat" with Raleigh, Beaumont, and Donne, or standing hatted in front of the Black Friars' Theatre, between a couple of his fellow-shareholders or fellow-actors? The costume of Shakespeare's time was certainly more picturesque than that prevailing in nineteenth-century New England. But are we to reject a rare picture of Hawthorne and his publishers, simply because we dislike the absurd tall silk hat of so-called modern civilization? By no means. The photograph may excite a smile, because "stove-pipe" hats are always and unchangeably a ridiculous outrage upon the innate dignity of man; but the smile cannot by any possibility detract from our respect for Hawthorne himself.

Lathrop's comments apply equally well to both photographs. Both show the same column, chair, and table as in the pose of Hawthorne seated, and in both, Hawthorne is holding a manuscript and looking to Fields at his right. In one photograph, however, the manuscript is held open, and in the other, it is held closed; Hawthorne is looking more directly at Fields, and both of them show a slight smile.

Both group poses have been published. A sepia reproduction of the closed manuscript pose appears in the Salem *Proceedings,* with the indication that it was made from a Black and Case print owned by Annie Fields, and Caroline Ticknor's *Hawthorne and His Publisher* includes a black and white copy. Julian Hawthorne published the open manuscript pose in *Hawthorne and His Circle,* and it was used in the *Critic* in 1904. Cartes of both poses with the Black imprint are in the Clark collection.[17]

The "Field Marshal" Photograph (1861)

A sixth photograph was probably taken in December 1861 by the third of Boston's major photographers, John A. Whipple. The evidence is unclear and at points contradictory, but according to Julian in his *Century* letter to Lathrop, "Previous to the Washington period a head, imperial size, was taken in Boston for Mr. Fields, and used to hang in his house; Fields called it the 'Field-Marshal Hawthorne,' from a certain military aspect it had." Identification follows from Julian's next comment: "It has since been copied, and there is an etching of it in the Biography"—meaning his own *Nathaniel Hawthorne and His Wife.* The Hawthorne portraits in that volume are three Schoff etchings—one based on the Osgood portrait, a second on the Mayall "Bright-Motley," and a third identified as Hawthorne at fifty-eight, "From a photograph taken in Boston." It is a bust etching showing the body turned to the left, with the head turned and looking to the front, and a lock of hair falling onto the forehead. As usual, Hawthorne is wearing a jacket, a shirt with a stand-up collar, and a bow tie. "S. A. Schoff aq fort" appears at the bottom, etched in the plate, both in the biography and in separately issued prints.

The etching appeared in later Houghton Mifflin publications and publications that cited permission from Houghton Mifflin, and the cut in the Salem *Proceedings* acknowledges as origin a photograph taken in Boston and owned by Annie Fields. A longer half-

Photograph of Hawthorne and his publishers Ticknor and Fields by James Wallace Black, 1861 or 1862. Courtesy of C. E. Frazer Clark, Jr.

Photograph of Hawthorne and his publishers Ticknor and Fields by James Wallace Black, 1861 or 1862. Courtesy of C. E. Frazer Clark, Jr.

length vignette showing more of the jacket, perhaps made from a heavily retouched photograph, was copyrighted in 1900 by E. A. Perry, issued as one of the "Perry Pictures," and published in the *Criterion* in 1904.

A second group of images in which Hawthorne looks much older apparently originates with the same "Field-Marshal" pose. When the Schoff etching is compared to the photogravure published in 1899 as the frontispiece to Annie Fields's memoir *Nathaniel Hawthorne*,

it seems apparent that the pose, clothing, moustache, and hair at the side of the head are identical, even to a curled lock near the right ear. However, in the photogravure, as well as in the identical cabinet-sized bust photograph issued by Notman Studios, the crown of Hawthorne's head is nearly bald. It seems likely that Schoff based his etching on a retouched photograph that added hair to Hawthorne's head or that he himself took the artistic liberty of adding the hair. The image in Annie Fields's *Hawthorne* is unequivocally identified. The attribution reads, "The photogravure used as a frontispiece to this volume is from a photo-

95

Etching by Stephen Alonzo Schoff, 1884. Prepared for Julian Hawthorne's *Nathaniel Hawthorne and His Wife.*

THE NOTMAN PHOTOGRAPHIC C⁰ LIMITED — 4 PARK ST. BOSTON.

Photograph by James Wallace Black or John Adams Whipple, 1861 or 1862. Called by Fields the "Field Marshal" pose. Cabinet-sized bust copy by Notman Studios. Courtesy of C. E. Frazer Clark, Jr.

graph taken about 1862 by J. W. Black, Boston"[18] and engraved by John Andrew and Son.

It seems probable that Fields's "head, imperial size" was made from an earlier photograph shortly after Hawthorne's death. But a series of letters from Sophia Hawthorne to Fields clearly indicates that it was not Black but John Adams Whipple who made it. Whipple, already a major photographer at the time of Hawthorne's 1848(?) daguerreotype, was still running a major establishment on Washington Street. His advertisements in the *Boston City Directory* specify a wide range of photographic services, including enlarging photographs and even making "life-size crayon photographs." Possibly Fields commissioned Whipple to do the imperial enlargement based on a Black original; although it is equally possible that Annie Fields was mistaken, and Whipple himself was also responsible for the original "Field Marshal" photograph. Sophia had com-

plained to Fields on 1 January 1862 that Silsbee's photographer was slower than Whipple; thus, Whipple might have taken the "Field Marshal" photograph some time before mid-December 1861.

In a series of four letters to Fields written just a few weeks after Hawthorne's death, Sophia ran the gamut of responses to the enlarged photograph ranging from delight to complete rejection. Her letter of 6 June 1864 begins by calling it "a very fine picture—a splendid head," and "a treasure," though Sophia insisted she loved "the one with a hat still better." The reference to Whipple's "superb picture" is ambiguous in this letter but clearer in the one written the following day. She asked Fields if she could "obtain of Whipple any more of the photographs which you call 'The Field Marshall' "; she wanted at least one for Julian.

But then four days later her attitude had changed. She still called the photograph a fine one but now declared that it was "not like him. All the light is left out of the face and it is heavy and massive. He does not seem to be in it....I think the head was fastened painfully back in the machine to keep it still." She complained that the figure appeared clumsy, but most important (and typically) she complained about the eyes, noting that she had "disliked them very much in the small head." She had tried to like the enlargement because Fields took "so much pains and care," and she felt "sad that Whipple has perhaps lost his own attempt"; but she declared that it would grieve her to become accustomed to this spiritless image. "When I first opened the package I was enchanted to see a head so large," she recalled, but size proved no virtue. "I hope you will not have it engraved but wait for the London one," she said. (The engraving of "the London one," Bright's photograph, proved equally displeasing.) Her letter the following day was brief and unequivocal: she "took out the picture, but liked it less than at first," and since the children shared her opinion, she would send the photograph back to Boston.

But Sophia's was the only real objection, and thirty years later the photograph was in good favor with family and friends. Annie Fields's frontispiece, engraved by John Andrew and Son of Boston, appeared in 1899, and a more sharply engraved portrait signed in the block by John Andrew had appeared two years earlier as a frontispiece to Rose Hawthorne Lathrop's *Memories of Hawthorne*. (John Andrew, the well-known Boston engraver frequently employed by Ticknor and Fields, had died in 1875, but his son John continued to use the old signature.) The same engraving was used as frontispiece to *The Hawthorne Centenary Celebrated at the Wayside*.[19] It was also issued as a separate black and white print, and the National Portrait Gallery owns a tinted version which shows a gray suit as well as yellow highlights in Hawthorne's hair. A variant

Engraving by John Andrew, 1897. Frontispiece to Rose Hawthorne Lathrop's *Memories of Hawthorne*.

engraving of the same solemn image is included in Caroline Ticknor's *Hawthorne and His Publisher*.

The grave "Field Marshal" pose might well be the one to which Hawthorne referred in what Fields called his "pleasant little note" of 14 November 1863. "Photographs of himself always amused him greatly," Fields said, then quoted from the note: "Here is the photograph,—a grandfatherly old figure enough; and I suppose that is the reason why you select it." Where Julian thought his father looked "military," Hawthorne simply thought he looked "grandfatherly." Hawthorne's next comment is slightly querulous, recalling his remarks about the Brady photograph a year and half earlier. He complained about portrayals of him even while acceding to public demand, saying, "I am much in want of *cartes-de-visite* to distribute on my own account, and am tired and disgusted with all the undesirable likenesses as yet presented of me." The rhetorical question which follows is nevertheless good-humored and even optimistic: "Don't you think I might sell my head to some photographer who would be willing to return me the value in small change; that is to say, in a dozen or two of cards?"[20]

There is no record that any photograph of Hawthorne was taken after he wrote this note, though earlier photographs remained in circulation, sometimes retouched, vignetted, or enlarged. Hawthorne's admirers can offer few complaints about the custom of head-selling and distributing "small change." Their sitter thought most photographs of him were "undesirable likenesses," and his wife was even harder to please; but the nine surviving photographs made in Boston and the four that would be taken in Washington together provide us with vivid images of Hawthorne as he moved to the end of his career—and the end of his life.

Notes

1. (Philadelphia, 1864), rpt. (Putney, Vt.; Helios, 1971), p. 379. George M. Silsbee had been in partnership with Marcus Masury since 1852 when in 1858 John Case joined the firm. Masury left in 1861; then in 1863 Silsbee left. Case and Getchell remained in partnership for two years; then from 1865 to 1866, Case was in partnership with Black. Thus, photographs with the Silsbee and Case imprint can probably be dated between 1861 and 1863, and those with the Case and Getchell imprint can probably be dated between 1863 and 1865. See Pamela Hoyle, *The Development of Photography in Boston*, p. 13, and *The Boston Ambience*, p. 10.

2. A copy of the small sixteen page pamphlet may be seen at the Massachusetts Historical Society.

3. *Ladies' Home Journal*, 11 (March 1894): 1–2.

4. *Memories*, p. 218.

5. (Cleveland: Rowfant Club, 1905).

6. Sophia's letter to Hawthorne, transcribed by Neal Smith, is in the Berg Collection. The Bradford "book" must have been an album of carte photographs.

7. Charles Henry Hart papers. Robinson was then treasurer of the Peabody Academy of Science.

8. Sophia's comment is reproduced in the catalogue for the 1904 Grolier Club exhibit of *First Editions of the Works of Nathaniel Hawthorne*, under the entry for a "Photograph of a Portrait in Crayon, by Samuel Worcester Rowse (b. 1822)," identified as "probably from the photograph described above"—correctly attributed though with wrong spelling and slightly incorrect date to "Silsbee, Cace & Co. (1862)."

9. As Buford Jones informs me, the *Yesterdays* chapter is a slightly revised version of the four installments of "Our Whispering Gallery" published in the *Atlantic Monthly* for February, March, April, and May 1871, framed by a nephew's visit to the "Gallery of Pictures" in Fields's "diminutive house." References to the Rowse portrait begin three of the four installments. A condensed version appeared in *Cornhill Magazine* in March, April, and May 1871. *Yesterdays* went through many editions after its first publication in 1872, and the Hawthorne chapter was issued as a separate volume in 1876.

10. *Harper's*, 89 (1894): 443. The comment is set into Howells's account of his first meeting with Hawthorne and his impression of a sympathetic "personage" dressed in black, his moustache still black and his eyes beautiful. The entire account was reprinted in *Literary Friends and Acquaintance* (New York: Harper, 1900).

11. The Salem *Proceedings* contains a list of "souvenirs" including a photograph of Una, Julian, and Rose taken by Silsbee and Case. It is almost certainly the same image. Another copy is preserved in the Hawthorne family album owned by Manning Hawthorne. I am grateful to Dora Golden's granddaughter Barbara Bacheler for copies of her Hawthorne photographs.

12. The pictures in the album were mounted as "medallions joined by a twisted band of enamelled flowers," Sophia explained, possibly the reason she used the phrase "Hawthorne flowers."

13. Root, pp. 371 and 381.

14. William Welling, *Photography in America: The Formative Years, 1839–1900*, p. 170.

15. The albumen print is on page 40 in an album presented to the Society by Mr. and Mrs. Alexander Calvin Washburn in 1893.

16. Charles Henry Hart Papers. The Salem photo-

grapher Frank Cousins made photographic copies of the Osgood and Healy portraits as well as a number of photographs and copyrighted his negatives. For a recent rendition of the bust image, see the frontispiece to Richard Harter Fogle, *Hawthorne's Imagery* (Norman, Okla.: University of Oklahoma Press, 1969).

17. The photograph is often reproduced and credited to Houghton Mifflin—for example, in Lloyd Morris, *The Rebellious Puritan: Portrait of Mr. Hawthorne* (New York: Harcourt Brace, 1927), and in Warren S. Tryon, *Parnassus Corner* (Houghton Mifflin, 1963). The firm of Houghton Mifflin retains only a copy of the original in its files. According to Yvonne Gunderson, Administrative Assistant to the President (in a letter of 26 September 1978), it is likely "that Houghton Mifflin did own the photograph earlier, but since then it has disintegrated through lack of care or has vanished because no one knew its worth." In his doctoral dissertation, "Two Partners in Boston: The Careers and Daguerreian Artistry of Albert Southworth and Josiah Hawes," University of Michigan, 1975, Charles LeRoy Moore includes the pose as Plate 2, assuming it is a Southworth and Hawes daguerreotype.

18. (Boston: Small and Maynard, 1899).

19. Edited by Thomas Wentworth Higginson (Boston: Houghton Mifflin, 1905).

20. Fields, pp. 111–12.

Photographs by Mathew Brady (1862)

On 31 March 1862, by appointment, Nathaniel Hawthorne and his friend and publisher William B. Ticknor walked into Mathew Brady's celebrated Gallery of Photographic Art in Washington. Hawthorne was gratified by the occasion, and even amused by it. He had been in the capital three weeks already; in the letter he wrote Sophia the next day, announcing that he would remain yet a week longer while Emanuel Leutze painted his portrait, he commented, "The world is not likely to suffer for lack of my likeness. I had a photograph of imperial size taken yesterday (a thirty-dollar photograph) and the artist promises to give me a copy." From the series of glass plate negatives taken that day, Hawthorne ordered several printed in the small format of cartes de visite to exchange with friends and acquaintances. Four poses survive from the occasion, two seated and two standing. But none of the results proved as pleasant as Hawthorne had anticipated.[1]

At this time, Mathew B. Brady (1823–1896) was the most famous photographer in the country, maintaining two establishments in New York, as well as the one in Washington.[2] Almost certainly, however, Brady was not in his Washington studio the day Hawthorne appeared. Brady had determined to embark on a massive coverage of the Civil War after he had photographed at Bull Run. Obtaining permission from Secretary of War Stanton, he spent the early months of 1862 organizing field units and training crews. On the first of April, accompanied by three photographers and his specially designed horse-drawn traveling darkrooms, he was at the wharves of Alexandria with McClellan's transports, heading down the Potomac for the beginning of the Peninsula Campaign, leaving his manager in charge of the Washington gallery.

Brady's studios in New York and Washington were all thriving at the time. A decade earlier he had won a medal at London's Crystal Palace photographic competition; he was celebrated, more recently, for portraits of Lincoln and the Prince of Wales, as well as for his early Civil War photographs. After beginning his career as a painter and lithographer, studying with William Page and Samuel F. B. Morse, Brady had become adept in the new technique of daguerreotypy. In 1844, he had established a daguerrean gallery in New York, later ventured a short-lived Washington gallery, and, in 1853, opened a second New York gallery. As new photographic techniques were developed, he applied them with remarkable success.

In 1856, Brady hired Alexander Gardner for his New York gallery, a man newly arrived from Scotland, trained in chemistry and physics, and skilled in the latest techniques of making wet plate collodion negatives as well as producing enlarged prints. It was no coincidence that soon after Gardner's arrival, Brady introduced his new "Imperial" photographs—17 x 21 inch prints often retouched with oils, crayons, ink, or watercolors, and selling for between fifty and seven hundred fifty dollars. In this context, Hawthorne's promised thirty dollar photograph was modest, though not of course when measured against the usual ten to twenty-five cent charge for an ordinary carte. Brady's pride in the Imperials is evident in his initial advertisement for the Washington Gallery of Photographic Art which he opened in 1858, stressing the availability of "the Imperial Photograph, hitherto made only at his well-known establishment in New York."[3]

Alexander Gardner was established from the start as manager of the Washington Gallery, responsible for all its operations, including bookings, printing, and purchases of equipment. A man of initiative and acumen, Gardner ordered new multi-lens cameras to facilitate producing inexpensive cartes de visite; and in 1861, he negotiated a profitable arrangement with the large New York firm of E. and H. T. Anthony, who not only sold photographic supplies but also made and sold prints for the escalating carte de visite trade. Gardner sold negatives of famous individuals to Anthony "after they had been used for the custom trade. Since there were usually several negatives for each exposure, this arrangement would not diminish the Brady operation's ability to keep turning out the same pictures, and Brady was still given credit on the back of the Anthony cards."[4] Thus, one of the Anthony cards in the collection of C. E. Frazer Clark, Jr., showing Hawthorne seated and with his jacket open, carries the imprint, "Published by E. ANTHONY/ 501 Broadway/ New York/ FROM/ PHOTOGRAPHIC NEGATIVE/ in/ BRADY'S/ National Portrait Gallery."

Celebrities such as Lincoln and Whitman felt gratified to be photographed at Brady's gallery in Washington, where Brady often posed them with the same armchair and marble-topped table evident in Hawthorne's photographs. Because Brady had a ready market for carte copies, he would often take photographs of the famous for little or no fee. His gallery was thronged with ordinary clients as well, however, most of them posing for their own inexpensive cartes. Brady thought cartes "cheapened his art," since only minimal retouching was possible on small negatives, but cartes were one of the firm's mainstays, selling tens of thousands each year.[5] A prominent customer would usually sit for a large portrait, which could be retouched and then rephotographed for cartes by Brady's highly trained employees. Even though Brady was troubled by failing eyesight and had to spend time in New York and on the battlefields, as well as in Washington, according to Meredith, "During the war, and until 1868 Brady, when he was not on the battlefields, photographed his most important clients."[6] But Hawthorne was not among them. Almost certainly it was Alexander Gardner who took the photograph of imperial size on 31 March 1862 and promised Hawthorne a copy.

As manager of Brady's Washington gallery, Gardner was usually behind the camera for celebrities when Brady was not. For years he had been frustrated by the relative anonymity of his role. In practice, every picture produced in a Brady studio or by a Brady employee bore the name of Mathew Brady, even photographs Gardner took on Civil War battlefields with his own equipment. His dissatisfaction with this practice culminated a month after Hawthorne's visit, when Gardner left Brady to become official photographer to the Army of the Potomac; and the following year he opened his own gallery.

Another ground for Gardner's dissatisfaction with Brady's practices may explain Hawthorne's problem with the promised "Imperial." Gardner was known as a strict businessman who disliked giving anything away. According to the Kunhardts, "Brady saw no need for a bookkeeper; Gardner insisted on one. Gardner would not offer discounts in return for sittings; Brady, facing intense competition from other photographers for celebrities, would have given away any number of pictures for the right to take them."[7] Thus, Brady's disgruntled manager would not have been happy to give something for nothing to Hawthorne, or to anyone else.

Gardner's original understanding with Hawthorne remains uncertain. As noted, Hawthorne had no doubt about getting the "Imperial"; he simply wrote Sophia, "the artist promises to give me a copy." Whether Gardner reneged on his promise is not clear, but Hawthorne was aware of a problem when he left Washington at the end of the week. After he returned to Concord and his copy had not arrived, he grew testy, and on 20 April he urged Ticknor to write to James Cephas Derby, a fellow-publisher who had been privy to arrangements for the session at Brady's.

I wish you would write to Derby about my large pho-

tograph. You know he promised me (and you too, for that matter) on behalf of Mr. Garden, that I should have a copy—which was my sole inducement for standing, because I knew that Mrs. Hawthorne would like to have it. But, on speaking to Garden about it, the day before I left Washington, it appeared to me that he did not intend it to give the copy.[8]

Ticknor presumably wrote to Derby, who in turn passed the complaint on to Robert S. Chilton, the friend who had made the arrangement with the Brady establishment. Over three months after his complaint to Ticknor, Hawthorne received a letter from Chilton, apologizing for the delay but promising delivery of the "Imperial." Chilton was not only a bureau head in the State Department but a friend of Derby, Leutze, and many other writers and artists in Washington. His letter of 31 July acknowledges that he had arranged for the Brady sitting (though he incorrectly stated its date) and expresses profound regret that a promise to him had been broken:

*On my return a month since from a brief absence in Europe, I was very much mortified to learn from my friend, M*r *Derby, that M*r *Brady's photographer in this city had failed to furnish you, as he had promised me to do, with a copy of the large-sized picture, which by his request & at my suggestion, you were kind enough to sit in April last. Indeed, I made it a condition of your coming to sit that he should give you a copy of the picture, & I therefore felt even indignant when I heard that this condition had been broken on his part. I am happy to state, however, that the matter has been explained to me, though not entirely to my satisfaction, and that a careful print of the negative photograph will soon be sent to you with a proper apology for its not having been furnished to you before.*

I feel sure you will hold me guiltless of any complicity in a circumstance which I fear may have occasioned you some little annoyance, and I beg you to believe that the occurrence has been a matter [that] has been to me a matter of sincere regret.[9]

The "matter" explained to Chilton undoubtedly involved Gardner's severed relationship with Brady. But

we may never know whether "a careful print of the negative photograph" ever reached Hawthorne.

Hawthorne did receive the cartes he had ordered almost immediately, and evidently he sent at least one vignetted pose home to Concord right away. A letter Una wrote her father from the Wayside, simply dated 3 April, seems to be a response to such a print: "Your picture we think is lovely that one that is a head only," she said. "Mamma says that it is one of the best, and I think so too."[10] Their praise remained unqualified even after Hawthorne's death. Sophia told Fields on 11 June 1864 that Una preferred the "Washington vignette" to the "Whipple" Imperial, agreed with Una that it would make a splendid engraving, and said Hawthorne "liked that best of all the American attempts."

At least at first, however, Hawthorne thought the photographs made his hair look too white. He evidently enclosed a carte with his letter to Fields of 2 April, announcing he would stay in Washington a few days longer for the Leutze sittings. His postscript makes a whimsical complaint: "My hair is not really so white as this photograph makes me; the sun seems to take an infernal pleasure in making me venerable—as if I were as old as himself."[11]

The following day he used almost the same words in a letter addressed to Professor Joseph Henry, the first Secretary of the Smithsonian Institution. During Hawthorne's four weeks in Washington, he was the guest of his old friend Horatio Bridge, then Chief of the Bureau of Provisions and Clothing of the Navy, and he became acquainted with other government officials such as Henry. The letter to him adopts a more courtly tone than the one to Fields, but the burden is the same: "I hope you will inform the ladies that my hair is not actually so white as these photographs would make it appear. The sun has an ill-natured pleasure, I believe, in making me look as old as himself." The pale vignetted bust Hawthorne sent Henry—now in the Clark collection—does indeed make Hawthorne's hair look whiter than in other photographs of the period. But of particular interest is Hawthorne's ease in playing the current game of exchanging cartes. He courteously responded to Henry's request, then courteously repeated his own: "I beg to remind you that you promised me, in exchange for my photograph, something much more

Photograph by Alexander Gardner for Mathew Brady, 1862. Front and back of carte de visite printed and distributed by E. and H. T. Anthony. Courtesy of C. E. Frazer Clark, Jr.

valuable—viz. your own."[12] Henry's compliance is evident from a letter Hawthorne wrote to Bridge on 13 April, soon after his return to Concord. "Yours, enclosing two photographs of Professor Henry, is received," the letter begins.

On 12 October, Hawthorne sent another carte to his London friend Francis Bennoch (who had just sent a picture of himself), slightly paraphrasing the complaints

about his hair already expressed to both Fields and Henry. "I send you a photograph of myself, taken four or five months ago. The sun has a grudge against me, and insists upon making my hair whiter than I see it in the glass, but that is no consequence. I am glad to see so little change in your own face, and likewise in Mrs. Bennoch...." In this case the carte was more than a cour-

Photograph by Alexander Gardner for Mathew Brady, 1862. Print from glass plate negative in collection of the National Archives (opposite).

teous exchange: it was a direct pictorial communication with a friend he never expected to see again.

Still another carte photograph was sent to the writer and former consular official, Donald G. Mitchell ("Ik Marvel"), along with a letter that provides specific information about the range of choices at Brady's. "The enclosed is the least objectionable of half a dozen from which I select it," Hawthorne said, "—all of them stern, hard, ungenial, and, moreover, somewhat grayer than the original." Mitchell reproduced the card photograph in his chapter on Hawthorne in *American Lands and Letters,* footnoting Hawthorne's comment. It is a pale and vignetted bust similar to the pose Hawthorne had sent to Henry, and presumably to Fields.[13]

From surviving Anthony cards of the "Brady" photographs by Gardner, it is clear that the bust reduction Hawthorne sent to Henry was made from a sitting pose, with Hawthorne's jacket unbuttoned. The card sent to Mitchell is essentially the same, but with the jacket buttoned. Presumably, the Brady photographs with which Julian Hawthorne was familiar were the seated poses. Echoing his father's criticism years later, Julian wrote to George Parsons Lathrop, "They were busts, carte-de-visite size, and show his hair and mustache nearly white."[14]

Caroline Ticknor also repeated Hawthorne's complaints about his hair's excessive whiteness in her comments on one of Hawthorne's standing photographs in *Hawthorne and His Publisher.* She first quoted Hawthorne's letter to Ticknor of 20 April 1862, which announced, "I brought home some of your standing photographs (of which see a specimen), as it was taken at the photographer's request, and there was nothing to pay. I hold them at your disposal." The syntax leaves it uncertain whether the specimen was of Ticknor or Hawthorne, but in either case, it is no surprise that the photographer had made the request or that "there was nothing to pay." Caroline Ticknor then commented on Brady's standing photographs of both men, calling them "admirable likenesses." However, she recorded Hawthorne's dismay about his own image: "Hawthorne looks perchance a bit ethereal and delicate (and he complained that his hair was 'too white')." Her father's standing photograph, she observed, made him look "somewhat stouter than ordinarily represented, having

declared about this time that he was adding too much to his weight." Nevertheless, she asserted, "both pictures are very characteristic of the subjects."[15]

It is not clear which of the two surviving standing photographs Caroline Ticknor knew, though perhaps it was the Napoleonic pose—a print often on display at the Wayside. According to the artist George H. Story, whose studios were in the same building as Brady's Washington gallery and who sometimes helped pose clients, "In those days, the photographer knew but one pose for a man to assume who was having his picture taken. He had to stand bolt upright with one hand thrust into the breast of his coat and the other on a table;—it was laughable, but it was the custom of the day."[16] In Hawthorne's Napoleonic pose, his left hand is behind his back, and the print shows the marble-topped table with a top hat on it and the carved chair evident in the seated photographs.

The second standing pose also shows Hawthorne's left hand behind his back, but his right hand is slightly extended. The vignetted plate in the collection of the Library of Congress shows evidence of retouching, and thus it is possible that it was intended for Hawthorne's promised "Imperial," the "careful print of the negative photograph" for which he endured the discomfort of a standing pose, "because I knew that Mrs. Hawthorne would like to have it."[17] But the "Imperial" has not turned up, and we may never know whether Sophia ever received the gift her husband planned.

What we do know is that he looked forward to a free "Imperial" that he perhaps never received and that despite his avowed dissatisfaction with the "half a dozen photographs" he was shown, he immediately ordered card-sized prints of two seated poses and sent them out to individuals he felt would like to own them. The episode sheds light on a few beguilingly human traits of Hawthorne's: his interest in receiving something for nothing (or rather, as a simple consequence of fame), his deprecation of his appearance, and—most surprising—his willingness to participate in the popular practice of promulgating and exchanging photographs.

When Hawthorne had first received Bridge's invi-

Photograph by Alexander Gardner for Mathew Brady, 1862. Copy of photograph at the Wayside National Historic Site (opposite).

tation to visit him in Washington, he had declined it on grounds of poor health, but his letter of refusal dated 13 February indicates that even then he was an old hand at the custom of exchanging cartes. He had written: "Meanwhile, I send you, enclosed, a respectable old gentleman, who, my friends say, is very like me, and may serve as my representative." Then, playing by the rules, he requested an exchange: "If you will send me a similar one of yourself, I shall be truly obliged."[18] As yet a further indication of his compliance with the photographic fad, he noted in a letter to Sophia dated 9 March 1862 that on a stroll he took in New York, "Nothing remarkable happened, save that my poor old bedevilled phizmahogany was seized upon and photographed for a stereoscope; and as far as I could judge from the negative, it threatens to be fearfully like." Unfortunately, there is no further information about the stereograph, and no print has been found.

But perhaps the fearful likeness increased Hawthorne's willingness to grant Brady's request for a sitting. Several weeks later he posed in the country's most famous photographic studio, though as it turned out he was not especially pleased with the results. He chose for reproduction the "least objectionable" of the portraits he considered "stern, hard, ungenial, and moreover, somewhat grayer than the original." Perhaps, as Hawthorne somewhat apologetically mailed out his Brady cartes, at a time when he felt dismayed by the Civil War and by his own difficulties in writing his romances, he felt a measure of vanity admixed with an intimation that the gray and ungenial image threatened even more than the New York stereograph to be "fearfully like." And, by contrast, his dismay at the ungenial Brady image helps us appreciate his unmitigated delight in the "aspect of immortal jollity" that Emanuel Leutze was then in the process of capturing on canvas.

Three of the four Brady poses are relatively accessible. The two seated poses, as well as the standing Napoleonic pose, were included in the Salem *Proceedings* and in subsequent volumes, usually accredited to the Bettman Archive or the Fredrick H. Meserve Col-

lection, and engravings of all three have been published. The seated pose with the coat unbuttoned was widely distributed as part of Brady's National Portrait Gallery, with countless carte copies sold by E. and H. T. Anthony. The first Brady image published in a periodical was the stern-faced wood engraving showing the image reversed, prepared by the German-born John Karst (1836–1932) from a drawing by H. L. Spread. It first appeared in *Appleton's Journal of Literature, Science, and Art* in 1870 and was reproduced in the *Critic* in 1881, 1894, 1897, and 1898.

Versions of the pose with the buttoned coat were more widely circulated. In 1887, Houghton Mifflin published a somewhat softened and sad-eyed bust engraving to accompany the two-page account of Hawthorne in a pamphlet intended for school use, *Portraits and Biographical Sketches of Twenty American Authors*.[19] Closer to the "ungenial" original is the engraving of the vignetted bust carte that Hawthorne gave to Donald Mitchell, published in *American Lands and Letters* in 1899. The heavily retouched cabinet print of the entire pose issued by Elliot and Fry of London, in the Clark collection, is an example of how photographers on both sides of the Atlantic appropriated prints made from original negatives. Two copies of the entire pose were published in 1904, the centenary of Hawthorne's birth: the halftone in the *Century* was engraved by Harry Davidson (1847–1924), an artist associated with the magazine for twenty-five years, and an unsigned photoengraving appeared in the *Critic*. A photograph made from the National Archives plate is reproduced as the frontispiece to the *Nathaniel Hawthorne Journal 1974,* and the Kunhardts reproduce a photograph from the Meserve Collection in *Mathew Brady and His World* (1977).

The standing poses are rarer than the ones with Hawthorne seated. A clumsy and almost unrecognizable oval bust print based on the Napoleonic pose appeared in the *Bookman* for 1897, signed "G. Reynolds. N.Y. 1887," and somewhat incorrectly identified as "From a wash drawing by G. Reynolds after a daguerreotype believed to have been taken in the last year of his life. Now reproduced for the first time." An accurate wood engraving of the entire pose appears in *American Lands and Letters*. A print of the photograph may

Photograph by Alexander Gardner for Mathew Brady, 1862. Print from glass plate negative. Courtesy of the Library of Congress (opposite).

be seen at the Wayside, and another is owned by Bowdoin College. The second standing pose, the rarest of all the Brady images, was published by James D. Horan as Plate 44 in *Mathew Brady: Historian with a Camera* (1955), identified as "a rare daguerreotype [*sic*] of Nathaniel Hawthorne. By Brady"; and a print made from a glass plate recently acquired by Frazer Clark is reproduced as the frontispiece to the *Nathaniel Hawthorne Journal 1972*.

Notes

1. This discussion was published in slightly different form in *Studies in the American Renaissance 1981* (Boston: Twayne, 1981), pp. 379–91.

2. Information about Mathew Brady and Alexander Gardner and about photographic processes comes from Roy Meredith, *Mr. Lincoln's Camera Man, Mathew Brady* (New York: Dover, 1974); James D. Horan, *Mathew Brady, Historian with a Camera* (New York: Crown, 1955); Kunhardt and Kunhardt, *Mathew Brady and His World;* and Gernsheim and Gernsheim, *The History of Photography*. The photographs of Hawthorne reproduced as cartes were taken with multi-lens cameras. This accounts for the plates of double lens exposures in the National Archives, the Library of Congress, and the National Portrait Gallery.

3. Kunhardt and Kunhardt, pp. 51–52.

4. Ibid., p. 55.

5. Ibid.

6. Meredith, p. 79.

7. Kunhardt and Kunhardt, p. 53.

8. James Cephas Derby (1818–1892) was the author of *Fifty Years Among Authors, Books, and Publishers* (Hartford, Conn.: M. A. Winter, 1885). Obviously Hawthorne was mistaken in his recollection of Gardner's name.

9. For a sketch of Chilton, see Derby, p. 640.

10. Only a single sheet of Una's letter is preserved in the Berg Collection of the New York Public Library. The hypothesis that she wrote to Hawthorne while he was in Washington is supported by the following sentences: "I am glad that our letters kept you alive[.] I thought that you would have too much to do to read them."

11. See the section on the Leutze portrait which follows.

12. This letter, as well as the carte sent to Henry, are in the collection of C. E. Frazer Clark, Jr.

13. Donald G. Mitchell, *American Lands and Letters: Leather-Stocking to Poe's "Raven"* (New York: Scribners, 1899), p. 261. I am grateful to Neal Smith for calling this to my attention.

14. "Some Portraits of Nathaniel Hawthorne," *Century,* 11(1887):899.

15. Caroline Ticknor, *Hawthorne and His Publisher* (Boston: Houghton Mifflin, 1913), pp. 280–81.

16. Meredith, p. 67.

17. Plates of this standing pose and of the two seated poses are part of the Brady-Handy Collection, Library of Congress, acquired from Brady's heirs in 1954. The National Archives also owns a plate of the seated pose with buttoned jacket.

18. Quoted by Derby, p. 633. See p. 104 above.

19. I am grateful to Buford Jones for calling my attention to this pamphlet, an "extra number" in the Riverside Literature Series, intended to provide schools with "some of the most interesting masterpieces of such writers as Longfellow, Holmes, Lowell, Hawthorne, etc." The account of Hawthorne is the eighth of twenty in the forty-two page pamphlet.

Oil Painting by Emanuel G. Leutze (1862)

The last oil portrait of Hawthorne was painted by Emanuel Gottlieb Leutze early in April 1862, near the end of Hawthorne's month-long visit to Washington with William Ticknor, and right after the Brady photographs were taken. It now hangs in the National Portrait Gallery. In several ways it is unusual: an oval, 35 x 30 inches, it shows Hawthorne facing almost directly forward, looking with robust good humor directly at the viewer, his eyes blue-gray, his hair dark brown but graying and trimly styled. The clothing is familiar: a black coat, vest, and cravat, and a high white collar. To the right of Hawthorne's shoulder, the can-

Oil painting by Emanuel Leutze, 1862. Courtesy of the National Portrait Gallery. Gift of Andrew W. Mellon, 1942 (opposite).

vas is signed, in red, "E Leutze." The critic Barbara Groseclose describes it vividly: "The oval bust stresses Hawthorne's blue eyes and high coloring, evoking in the smoothly contoured yet robust painted features a sense of the novelist's romantic nature and New England freshness."[1]

Hawthorne wrote of his first meeting with Leutze in "Chiefly About War Matters," printed in the July 1862 issue of the *Atlantic*. He and Ticknor had ventured to the Capitol in search of the renowned painter who was working on his large allegorical and historical mural, "Westward the Course of Empire." Hawthorne was quickly convinced that the work was "emphatically original and American," and he praised the painter as a genial individual "of Teutonic build and aspect, with an ample beard of a ruddy tinge and chestnut hair," who seemed "satisfactorily adequate to the business which brought him thither." Hawthorne's pleasure in the artist and his work alleviated his depression about America's "dismal time" of civil war. Leutze's optimistic and energetic conception seemed a "good augury," while his calm diligence "was an absolute comfort." Applying aesthetic standards developed during his years abroad, Hawthorne extolled Leutze for "beautifying and idealizing our rude, material life," and for producing art "rich in thought and suggestiveness." The comforting thought that "Westward the Course of Empire" suggested to him was that Americans "have an indefeasible claim to a more enduring national existence."[2]

Leutze must have enjoyed his encounter with such a sympathetic spectator; he immediately prevailed on Hawthorne to sit for a portrait. On 1 April, Hawthorne informed Sophia that he would stay in Washington longer than he intended, "for Leutze wishes to paint a portrait of me, and is to have the first sitting to-day." He did not expect a long delay, however: "Three or four sittings will finish it, no doubt; so that I expect to start for home early in next week." Apparently his own willingness to extend his visit surprised him: "I little thought to have made so long a stay, when I left the Wayside," he said.

His letter to Fields the following day seems apologetic, yet pleased, about the sittings. "I stay here only while Leutze finishes a portrait—which I think will be the best ever painted of the same unworthy subject,

and so does Ticknor," he wrote. Clearly, he had enjoyed his initial sitting, and his reaction to the artist's convivial solicitude seemed to guarantee that Leutze's portrait would be "the best."

One charm it must needs have—an aspect of immortal jollity and well-to-doness; for Leutze, when the sitting begins, gives me a first-rate cigar, and when he sees me getting tired, he brings out a bottle of splendid champagne; and we quaffed and smoked, yesterday, in a blessed state of mutual good-will, for three hours and a half, during which the picture made a really miraculous progress.

Evidently James and Annie Fields had met Leutze, since Hawthorne commented, "Leutze speaks most kindly of you and admiringly of Mrs. Fields." He concluded unequivocally, "He is the best of fellows."

At the time Hawthorne met him, Emanuel Leutze (1816–1868) was at the height of his powers. A German immigrant, he began his career as a portrait painter in Philadelphia, then returned to Germany in 1840, maintaining a studio in Dusseldorf for twenty years. After winning world renown for his painting of "Washington Crossing the Delaware," he returned to America in 1859, commissioned to paint "Westward the Course of Empire" for the House of Representatives. During his last years he painted a series of portraits of American statesmen and creative artists, Hawthorne among them. Groseclose speaks of Leutze's "unerring ability to convey the personality of his sitter," and he does present Hawthorne's characteristic alertness and composure; but Leutze is the only painter to show him in a genial mood, with a twinkle in his eyes.

Leutze's interest in Hawthorne had begun at least as early as 1850, when his friend Abraham Cozzens sent him *The Scarlet Letter* as a gift, prompting his painting of "Hester Prynne and Little Pearl." James T. Fields saw the painting on a visit to Cozzens's house in New York in 1851, and wrote to tell Hawthorne it was a "great picture" which he should try to see. Hawthorne and Leutze might well have spoken of this picture in the "blessed state of mutual good-will" which prevailed during Hawthorne's sittings. Clearly, Hawthorne "took a special fancy to the artist," as Fields commented, but

White-line wood engraving by R. G. Tietze, 1894. Published in the *Century*.

the relationship apparently terminated with the sittings.[3]

"While he [Hawthorne] was in Washington, the artist Leutze made an oil-portrait of him, which those who have seen it pronounce good," Julian wrote Lathrop in 1887, adding correctly, "This has never been reproduced."[4] Evidently Julian had not yet seen the portrait itself; in *Nathaniel Hawthorne and His Wife* he had said he did not know what had become of it. By the time he wrote *Hawthorne and His Circle*, however, he had seen the painting and found he disliked it. "Except photographs, no really good likeness of my father was ever taken," he asserted. "The portrait painted in Washington, in 1862, by Leutze, was the least successful of them all."[5] Perhaps Julian was disconcerted to see his father with an uncharacteristically jovial demeanor.

The journey of the Hawthorne portrait from Leutze's studio to the walls of the National Portrait Gallery is almost completely documented. It was in the artist's collection until his death in 1868. In March 1869, it was sold at auction in New York, when John Kensett bought it. A Mrs. W. H. Osborn owned the portrait in 1894. That year, a white-line wood engraving by Richard George Tietze (fl. 1880–1905) first appeared in the *Century,* signed in the block "R. G. Tietze," and Mrs. Osborn was identified as owner of the painting. Prof. Henry F. Osborn owned it at least between 1904 and 1915; then a Perry Osborn sold it to Thomas B. Clarke in 1923. During the years 1923–1931 it was exhibited in the Philadelphia Museum of Art. Andrew Mellon was the next owner; in 1942, the Mellon Trust gave it to the National Gallery of Art, and since 1965, it has been in the possession of the National Portrait Gallery.[6] The portrait was reproduced in the Salem *Proceedings* and in several recent exhibition catalogues, including the National Portrait Gallery's *This New Man* in 1968; and Groseclose includes it in her article on Leutze. Tietze's engraving appeared in the *Century* for 1904 as well as 1894.

The granite bust of Hawthorne by J. S. Hartley on the portico of the Library of Congress seems in its frontality, billowing hairline, and slightly furrowed brow to be based on the Leutze painting, although its more serious visage is closer to the Silsbee and Case photographs. According to an 1896 issue of *Harper's Weekly,*[7] Jonathan Scott Hartley had recently completed clay models of three "heroic-sized busts" representing "three splendid types of American men of letters"— Emerson, Irving, and Hawthorne—and the three undraped busts were already carved in granite. Hartley (1845–1912), born in Albany and trained under Erasmus Palmer, was nationally renowned for his portrait busts; and for the Library commission, he had "been able to work after authoritative portraits, and in each case to secure a likeness that admits of no doubt." Hartley's three busts are part of a group of nine on the facade, each three feet tall and each set off by a rounded window in the granite wall of the Library.

Notes

1. Barbara S. Groseclose, "Emanuel Leutze: portraitist," *Antiques,* 102 (November 1975): 986–91.

2. From The Riverside Edition of *The Complete*

Oil painting of "Washington Irving and His Literary Friends at Sunnyside" by Christian Schussele (second version, 1864) based on composite india ink drawing by F. O. C. Darley (1860). Courtesy of the National Portrait Gallery.

Works of Nathaniel Hawthorne, 12 vols. (Boston: Houghton Mifflin, 1887–1888) XII: 305–7.

3. In "Nathaniel Hawthorne and Emanuel Leutze," *Essex Institute Historical Collections,* 118 (1982): 67–91, Sterling Eisiminger and John L. Idol, Jr., present details about Leutze's painting of "Hester Prynne and Little Pearl" (now lost)—including a fabrication by Leutze about the occasion which inspired it, and his later comment that he had done the painting as soon as Cozzens sent *The Scarlet Letter:* "I made a myth of it and succeeded in agreeably surprising both him and Mr. Hawthorne." See Fields, p. 96.

4. Quoted in "Portraits." Possibly Julian came to know the portrait through the Tietze engraving in 1894.

5. NHW, II: 309; *HC,* p. 312.

6. Most details of ownership are recorded in the Catalog of American Portraits and in the Frick Art Reference Library.

7. *Harper's Weekly,* 9 (1896): 1043.

"Washington Irving and His Literary Friends at Sunnyside" (1863)

By November 1860, Felix Octavius Carr Darley (1822–1888) had already started to plan his large composite india-ink drawing of "Washington Irving and His Literary Friends at Sunnyside," requesting sittings or photographs from the writers he had been commissioned by the Derby Galleries to portray. By this time, Darley was well established as a fine book illustrator and one of the country's best draftsmen. Longfellow readily agreed to sit for him and to negotiate for photographs of Hawthorne, Emerson, and several others.[1] Hawthorne had recently returned from England, and possibly Longfellow had heard about the Mayall photographs and managed to procure prints of one or more poses for Darley (perhaps from Henry Bright, who was one of his correspondents). No copy of Darley's drawing is available, and we cannot ascertain whether the artist worked from a Mayall photograph of Hawthorne or perhaps a later photograph negotiated by Longfellow and now lost. But the oil painting based on the composite drawing and the engraving of the painting suggest that Darley made the first American portrait of Hawthorne with a moustache.

Irving had died in 1859, and in his honor the Derby Galleries not only commissioned Darley's ambitious drawing but planned an oil painting and an engraving based on it, on the model of such commercially successful prints as "Walter Scott and His Friends." The painter Derby chose was the Alsatian-born Philadelphia painter and engraver, Christian Schussele (1824 or 1826–1879), and the engraver was Thomas Oldham Barlow of London. But it would be over three years before their works were completed.

Not until December 1863 was Schussele's large canvas—4 x 6 feet—exhibited at the Derby Galleries, first "by invitation to a number of leading connoisseurs, artists, &c.," and then to the general public. Reviewers from the city's newspapers agreed it was excellent, truthful, and charming—"without doubt, the best national picture ever painted in America," said the *Brooklyn Daily Union*. They all noted that the Barlow engraving—21½ x 31 inches on a 31 x 43-inch sheet—was nearing completion after three years, and the Irving Publishing Company of 625 Broadway (the same address as the Gallery) offered it to subscribers for prices ranging from $10 a print to $50 for an artist's proof. "In its production no expense has been spared," the publishers announced. "It is engraved on steel, in the highest style of the art, known as mixed line and stipple, by Thomas Oldham Barlow of London, from the

Ivory miniature by Peter Kramer, 1862 or after. Courtesy of the George A. Plimpton Collection, Rare Book and Manuscript Library, Columbia University.

original and spirited design by F. O. C. Darley, the great American artist."

As part of the same event, the publishers issued a pamphlet entitled *Sketches of Distinguished American Authors, Represented in Darley's New National Picture, Entitled Washington Irving and His Literary Friends, at Sunnyside*, affirming that "the production of this charming picture will be universally regarded as a National event." The introduction described Hawthorne as apparently "already wandering in imagination" through Irving's house, and the pamphlet included a two and a half page biographical sketch of Hawthorne.[2]

In the composition itself, the bust of Hawthorne is a

relatively unobtrusive part of the design: he is in the background, fifth from the left, wearing a jacket with high-collared shirt and bow-tied stock. But Darley dramatized the head by placing it against a pillar, inclined down and to the right (away from Irving). Darley was praised for his relaxed harmonious composition of credibly portrayed individuals, and the painting and engraving that followed his design suggest that he gave his portrait of Hawthorne a characteristically meditative (if somewhat sarcastic) expression.

Within a year, Schussele produced a second version of his group painting, virtually identical to the first. This almost unknown painting—measuring 52 x 78 inches and signed and dated 1864—has recently been acquired by the National Portrait Gallery.

Schussele's original painting hangs at Sunnyside, Irving's home in Tarrytown, New York; and copies of the Barlow engraving are in the collections of the Massachusetts Historical Society, the National Portrait Gallery, and the Essex Institute. But I find no evidence of what happened to Darley's original drawing.

Notes

1. "...illustrated by Darley": An Exhibition of Original Drawings by the American Book Illustrator Felix Octavius Carr Darley (1822–1888), May 4–June 18, 1978 (Wilmington, Delaware: The Museum, 1978), pp. 16–17. Longfellow's letter to Darley is quoted in the Stanislaus Henkels Catalogue for the Davis and Harvey Auction Rooms (Philadelphia, 1908), p. 7, item 1048. In his journal for 1 November 1860, Longfellow reported, "Had my photograph taken for Darley to go into a picture he is making, 'Washington Irving and his friends'" (Manuscript at Houghton Library, Harvard). Darley illustrated Longfellow's "Evangeline" in 1866 and dedicated his 1879 volume of illustrations for The Scarlet Letter to Longfellow.

2. I am grateful to Georgia Bumgardner of the American Antiquarian Society for supplying me with xeroxes of the Irving Publishing Company's announcement of the Barlow engraving, the relevant sections of their Sketches of Distinguished American Authors, and the newspaper reports about the Schussele painting and the entire "Washington Irving" project. The New York Herald said Darley "had the advantage of sittings from all the living authors represented," and the New York Daily Times said "Special photographs were taken of all the leading characters; each individual being placed in the exact position required by Mr. Darley."

Ivory Miniature by Peter Kramer (1862 or after)

A miniature watercolor portrait of Nathaniel Hawthorne delicately painted on ivory by Peter Kramer is now in the possession of Columbia University, part of the Plimpton Collection in Butler Library. It is a mounted oval, about 5 x 3 inches, predominantly in light sepia tones with details picked out in darker tones of gray, and with a very pale blue wash both in the background and highlighting the clothing. The painting is signed "P Kramer," and the label identifies the artist as Peter Kramer and gives the date "about 1859." It was probably actually painted several years later. The Bavarian-born painter and lithographer, Peter Kramer (1823–1907) came to the United States in 1848 and worked in Philadelphia until 1871, then (after an interlude in Munich) in New York City. Details in Kramer's painting such as the figure's receding hairline, his clothing, and the column in the background all appear in photographs made of Hawthorne in Boston around 1862. Kramer might have worked from one or more of those photographs, though possibly Hawthorne posed for the miniature during his stop in Philadelphia in March 1862 or during his final visit in April 1864.

Apocryphal Likenesses

Oil Sketch by Henry Inman? (1835)

The Essex Institute owns a rough oil sketch, 7 x 6 inches, supposedly a portrait of Nathaniel Hawthorne painted by Henry Inman (1801–1846), made in Boston in 1835. The bust portrait shows a young man facing right but looking left, with a drooping moustache and thick brown hair, wearing a black coat and a black ascot under an open-collared white shirt. Aside from the fact that we have no proof that Hawthorne wore a moustache as a young man, the sketch bears only slight resemblance to known Hawthorne portraits. Further, art historian William H. Gerdts says unequivocally that the painting is not by Inman and that it has a "uniquely grand spurious pedigree."[1]

Silhouette of Sophia and Nathaniel Hawthorne by Auguste Edouart (1843)

The Essex Institute owns a silhouette purportedly of "Mr. and Mrs. Nathaniel Hawthorne of Salem, Mass.," on which is written, in handwriting of the period, "Aug' Edouart fecit Boston 1843." However, the man in the silhouette is bearded, the lady is elaborately coiffed, and the formally garbed figures bear no resemblance to the Hawthornes. Further, Andrew Oliver, author of the definitive study of the silhouettes of Auguste E. Edouart (1784–1861), knows of no silhouette of Hawthorne ever cut by Edouart, though he did make thousands during his decade in America. According to Oliver, Edouart had worked in Boston in 1842, but the list of known silhouettes cut during 1843 precludes his being in the Boston area that year. The final argument is visual. It is inconceivable, as Oliver agrees, that Hawthorne should "appear with a beard."[2]

Marble Bust by Preston Powers (1875)

The Boston Museum of Fine Arts owns a marble bust thought to be of Nathaniel Hawthorne, inscribed with Powers's name and the date 1875. It is a three-quarters bust in the neoclassic style, 27 inches high, with the head turned slightly right and the body draped in a toga. The sculptor, Preston Powers (1843–aft. 1925), was born in Florence, studied with his father, and worked in Boston and Washington as well as in Florence. The "Hawthorne" bust, at one time owned by Mrs. George Waldo Emerson, was given to the Museum in the 1960s by Maxim Karolik, a pioneer collector of American art. A curator at the Museum suggests, "probably Powers modelled the bust in clay during Hawthorne's lifetime—or perhaps based the work on a well-known photograph or painting of him, and transferred the clay bust to marble at a later period," but "there is no record in the Powers' papers of either Hiram or his son Preston ever having received a commission for Hawthorne's portrait."[3] It is certainly true that Hawthorne was a good friend of Hiram Powers during his residence in Florence in 1858, when Preston was fifteen, and it is possible that Preston made drawings or a clay model of Hawthorne at that time, which he subsequently worked into marble. In 1875, it would have been even more likely for him to work from one of the many known Hawthorne portraits. In any event, the moustached face with set lips and staring eyes resembles Mark Twain or William Faulkner as much as it does Hawthorne, and the large and pendulous earlobes, the short-cropped curly hair, and the low browline are surely not those of Nathaniel Hawthorne.

Notes

1. Letter from William H. Gerdts, 5 July 1979.
2. Letter from Andrew Oliver, 5 August 1979.
3. Letter from Jan Seidler, 1 December 1979.

Afterword

"Nothing, in the whole circle of human vanities, takes stronger hold of the imagination, than this affair of having a portrait painted. Yet why should it be so? The looking-glass, the polished globes of the andirons, the mirror-like water, and all other reflecting surfaces, continually present us with portraits, or rather ghosts of ourselves, which we glance at, and straightway forget them. But we forget them, only because they vanish. It is the idea of duration—of earthly immortality—that gives such a mysterious interest to our own portraits."

(*"The Prophetic Pictures," **Twice-told Tales**, p. 173*)

Hawthorne's remarks about the British historical portraits he saw at the Manchester Arts Exhibition in the summer of 1857 sum up his reservations about portraiture in general. Looking at the "cold and stiff" older portraits and the newer ones that seemed devoid of both truth and beauty, he said, "I have a haunting doubt of the value of portrait-painting; that is to say, whether it gives you a genuine idea of the person purporting to be represented." Presumably, he included himself.

He also complained that "a full length portrait has seldom face enough," that "the artist does not often find it possible to make the face so intellectually prominent as to subordinate the figure and the drapery." Even worse, some artists flattered their sitters, some abided by ephemeral standards of taste, and others projected themselves onto the canvas. Hawthorne said in summation, "Considering how much of his own conceit the artist puts into a portrait, how much affectation the sitter puts on, and then again that no face is the same to any two spectators; also, that these portraits are darkened and faded with age, and can seldom be more than half seen, being hung too high, or some-

how or other inconvenient—on the whole, I question whether there is much use in looking at them" (*EN*, p. 552). Reading these reservations prompts us to reconsider why Hawthorne had at this time already sat for his portrait and would do so again.

One obvious answer is that whether by his own design or because of the period taste, all of his portraits have "face enough"—that is, in all of them the face is "intellectually prominent," and we are only minimally aware of "the figure and the drapery." For another, as far as we know, he respected those who portrayed him, particularly Thompson and Leutze; they seemed more interested in truth than in flattery or fashion. Surely he presented himself without affectation. And his conclusion that "no face is the same to any two spectators" could turn the risk of portraiture into a kind of game. That his portraits might deteriorate or be improperly displayed never seemed to concern him.

Yet in a sense, he was playing the same double game with his portraits that he did with his fiction and within his fiction, trying to open an intercourse with the world and yet remain elusive. Even though he was known to slip out the back door of the Old Manse of the Wayside when an admirer approached, he liked the idea of being a literary personage. And even though he mistrusted portraits, he wanted their form of earthly immortality.

Thus, he would probably be glad to know that all of his oil portraits have been cleaned and that all are well displayed. It would probably amuse him, however, to know that Kuntze's plaster bas relief sits in a crowded storeroom at the New-York Historical Society and that there seems to be no trace of the marble medallion. He would probably accept philosophically the disappearance of the Southworth miniature, the miniature made for Charlotte Cushing, the daguerreotypes "seized" in 1852, the drawing by Miss Hawarth, whatever portrait busts were made in Rome after Lander's, and the New York "stereoscope." And he might be diverted by disputes about the Mayall photographs, the Bowdoin silhouette, the moustached miniature, and the apocryphal portraits. On the other hand, he might be taken aback by the sale of postcards and lacquered boxes displaying the Osgood portrait at the Essex Institute.

But he would probably approve the approach to "a genuine idea" of him that the surviving portraits permit. Through them he tacitly admits us to acquaintance, while concealing his "inmost Me." Looking at them is like watching a kind of moving picture that displays what he might call his "characteristics" and "remarkables," and hints at his complexities and inner mysteries. The surveyor Hawthorne is himself surveyed. Although Fields was undoubtedly correct in stating that "it was impossible for art to give the light and beauty of his wonderful eyes," nevertheless, those eyes repeatedly look out at us from a face whose lines gradually slacken, sometimes sorrowful but always attentive, and the kind viewer can respond to them as Hawthorne's kind reader to his fiction, contemplating what proved transient but also what remained constant in his life and in his career.

Glossary

Albumen print

Introduced *circa* 1850 for use with wet collodion plates, (see below) and made commercially available between 1850 and 1855, albumen-coated paper prints were used almost exclusively until the 1880s and were thus the medium for most Victorian photographic portraits. Paper that had been dried and stored after floating in a solution of albumen and salt was chemically sensitized, exposed, and printed, and then permanently fixed, toned, and cut to size. Color ranged from light yellow to rich chocolate, and surfaces ranged from a slight sheen to a high gloss. As the print was thin, it was usually mounted on a card as a cabinet photograph or a carte de visite (see below).

Cabinet photograph

A portrait albumen print, usually around 4 x 5½ inches on a thick cardboard mount of 4¼ x 6½ inches. It was introduced in 1866 and remained popular until the end of the century.

Carte de visite (or carte)

The cheapest and most popular form of photographic portrait, an albumen paper print usually 2¼ x 3½ inches and mounted on a 2½ x 4-inch card. With multilens cameras and movable plateholders, generally eight but as many as twelve images could be imprinted on a single glass plate negative. Therefore, cartes could be produced quickly and cheaply and averaged about four dollars per dozen. Cartes were introduced in the late 1850s, remained popular for over twenty years, and were often collected in albums.

Daguerreotype

The first practical photographic process, announced in 1839 by L. J. M. Daguerre and soon produced throughout the western world. In this so-called "sun-drawn picture" or "mirror with a memory," a sitter's image was reflected onto a silvered and sensitized metal plate set into a camera obscura fitted with a lens; it was then exposed, developed by exposure to mercury vapor, fixed, washed, and sealed into a frame whose glass protected it from damage. The daguerreotype is a singular and unique image on a mirrored surface, preserving the sitter's appearance in detail but reversed, as in a mirror. The customer could choose the size and frame and decide whether to have the image colored. Since a sitter had to remain still for about thirty seconds, poses were stiff and stereotyped, often sustained by a special chair with headclamps, and an operator often used a skylight to reduce exposure time. Thus, the daguerreotype was fairly expensive: a half-plate such as Hawthorne's would cost around four dollars, and by the mid 1850s, when less expensive albumen prints were readily available, it had radically declined in popularity.

Engraving

The preparation of a printing surface by incising lines or dots on a metal plate which is then inked and printed in an intaglio process (or a print resulting from that process). An engraving to be included with a published book, such as Phillibrown's portrait of Hawthorne, was separately printed and bound in.

Etching

The preparation of a coated metal printing surface by baring lines, dots, or surfaces, then immersing the plate in acid to "bite" the exposed areas, after which the plate is inked and printed in an intaglio process (or a print resulting from that process). An etching included in a published book, such as Schoff's portraits of Hawthorne, was separately printed and bound in.

Line engraving

The engraving process, plate, or print that uses only pure black lines or dots.

Wet collodion negative

A process introduced in 1851 and widely used for twenty-five years. Collodion—a solution of gun-cotton in acidified ether with added iodide—was poured onto glass to give an even surface, after which the plate was dipped into a silver nitrate solution, then loaded into a camera darkslide while still wet, and brought to the camera. The plate remained wet during exposure (lasting from seconds to minutes) and development, after which it was rinsed, fixed, and dried, and ready for printing.

White-line wood engraving

A relief process wood block in which flicks and dots are removed in varying depths and dimensions to create subtle effects of texture and lighting and which is then inked and printed (or the print resulting from that process). Magazine portraits of Hawthorne in the 1880s, such as those of Timothy Cole, were often white-line engravings.

Wood engraving

A relief process in which an endgrain boxwood block is incised, excavating all that is to remain white and leaving what is to remain black, after which the block is inked and printed (or the print resulting from that process). Since woodblocks could be joined in forms with type and inked and printed simultaneously, they were inexpensive modes of reproduction. The earliest published periodical portraits of Hawthorne were wood engravings.

Selected Bibliography

Clark, C. E. Frazer, Jr. "A Lost Miniature of Nathaniel Hawthorne." *Nathaniel Hawthorne Journal 1976*, pp. 81–86.

———. *Nathaniel Hawthorne: A Descriptive Bibliography*. Pittsburgh: University of Pittsburgh Press, 1978.

Craven, Wayne. *Sculpture in America*. New York: Thomas Y. Crowell, 1968.

Fields, James T. *Yesterdays with Authors*. Boston: James R. Osgood, 1872.

Gernsheim, Helmut, and Alison Gernsheim. *The History of Photography*. New York: McGraw-Hill, 1969.

Groce, George C., and David A. Wallace. *The New-York Historical Society's Dictionary of Artists in America, 1564–1860*. New Haven, Conn.: Yale University Press, 1957.

Hall, Robert C. "Scrapbook of *Hawthorne's Portraits, 1886–87*," in the Berg Collection, New York Public Library.

Harwell, Richard. *Hawthorne and Longfellow: A Guide To An Exhibit*. Brunswick, Me.: Bowdoin College, 1966.

Hawthorne, Julian. *Hawthorne and His Circle*. New York: Harper, 1903.

———. *Nathaniel Hawthorne and His Wife*. 2 vols. Boston: James R. Osgood, 1884.

———. "The Portraits of Hawthorne." *New York World*, 26 June 1886.

Hawthorne, Nathaniel. *The Centenary Edition of the Works of Nathaniel Hawthorne*. Edited by William A. Charvat *et al.* (18 vols. projected) Columbus, Ohio: Ohio State University Press, 1962– .

———. "Chiefly About War Matters," *in The Complete Works of Nathaniel Hawthorne*. Edited by George P. Lathrop. 12 vols. Boston: Houghton Mifflin, 1887–1888. 12:299–345.

———. *The English Notebooks*. Edited by Randall Stewart. New York: Modern Language Association of America, 1941.

———. *Hawthorne's Lost Notebook: 1835–1841*. Transcript by Barbara S. Mouffe. University Park, Pa.: Pennsylvania State University Press, 1978.

Healy, George P. A. *Reminiscences of a Portrait Painter*. Chicago: McClurg, 1894.

Horan, James B. *Mathew Brady: Historian with a Camera*. New York: Crown, 1955.

Hoyle, Pamela. *The Boston Ambience: An Exhibition of Nineteenth-Century Photographs*. Boston: The Boston Athenaeum, 1981.

———. *The Development of Photography in Boston, 1840–1975*. Boston: The Boston Athenaeum, 1979.

Hull, Raymona. "Nathaniel Hawthorne and Francis Bennoch." *Nathaniel Hawthorne Journal 1974*, pp. 48–74.

Idol, John, Jr., and Sterling Eisiminger. "Hawthorne Sits for a Bust by Maria Louisa Lander." *Essex Institute Historical Collections* 114 (1978): 207–12.

Jussim, Estelle. *Visual Communication and the Graphic Arts: Photographic Technologies in the Nineteenth Century*. New York: R. R. Bowker, 1974.

Kunhardt, Dorothy Meserve, and Philip B. Kunhardt, Jr. *Mathew Brady and His World*. Alexandria, Va.: Time-Life, 1977.

Lathrop, George Parsons. "Biographical Sketch of Nathaniel Hawthorne," in *The Complete Works of Nathaniel Hawthorne*. Edited by George P. Lathrop. 12 vols. Boston: Houghton Mifflin, 1887–1888, 12:441–569.

——. "Some Portraits of Hawthorne." *Century* 11 (April 1887): 895–99.

Lathrop, Rose Hawthorne. *Memories of Hawthorne.* Boston: Houghton Mifflin, 1897.

——. "My Father's Literary Methods." *Ladies' Home Journal* 11 (May 1894): 1–2.

Leach, Joseph. *Bright Particular Star: The Life and Times of Charlotte Cushman.* New Haven, Conn.: Yale University Press, 1970.

de Mare, Marie. *G. P. A. Healy, American Artist.* New York: David McKay, 1954.

Mellow, James. *Nathaniel Hawthorne in His Times.* Boston: Houghton Mifflin, 1980.

Meredith, Roy. *Mr. Lincoln's Camera Man.* New York: Scribner's, 1946.

Mott, Frank Luther. *History of American Magazines.* 5 vols. Cambridge, Mass.: Harvard University Press, 1930–1968.

Newhall, Beaumont. *The Daguerreotype in America.* New York: Duell, Sloan and Pearce, 1961.

Peabody, Elizabeth. "The Hawthorne Photograph." *Salem Gazette,* 31 August 1886.

The Proceedings In Commemoration of the One Hundredth Anniversary of the Birth of Nathaniel Hawthorne, Held at Salem Massachusetts, June 23, 1904. Salem, Mass.: Essex Institute, 1904.

Robinson, William T. *A Certain Slant of Light: The First Hundred Years of New England Photography.* Boston: New York Graphic Society, 1980.

Root, Marcus Aurelius. *The Camera and the Pencil.* Philadelphia, 1864. Rpt. Putney, Vt.: Helios, 1971.

Sharf, Frederick A. "Charles Osgood: The Life and Times of a Salem Portrait Painter." *Essex Institute Historical Collections* 102 (1966): 203–12.

——. " 'A More Bracing Atmosphere': Artistic Life in Salem, 1850–1859." *Essex Institute Historical Collections* 95 (1959): 149–64.

Sobieszek, Robert A., and Odette M. Appel. *The Spirit of Fact: The Daguerreotypes of Southworth and Hawes, 1843–1862.* Boston: D. R. Godine, 1976.

Taft, Robert. *Photography and the American Scene: A Social History, 1838–1889.* New York: Macmillan, 1938.

Tharp, Louise Hall. *The Peabody Sisters of Salem.* Boston: Little, Brown, 1950.

Ticknor, Caroline. *Hawthorne and His Publisher.* Boston: Houghton Mifflin, 1913.

Weitenkampf, Frank. *American Graphic Arts.* New York: Macmillan, 1924.

——. "Portraits and Other Illustrations," in "List of Books...By and Relating to Nathaniel Hawthorne." *Bulletin of the New York Public Library* 7 (July 1904): 513–14.

Welling, William. *Photography in America: The Formative Years, 1839–1900.* New York: Thomas Y. Crowell, 1978.